# HE SPEAKS
## TO ME EVERYWHERE

# HE SPEAKS
## TO ME EVERYWHERE

*Meditations on Christianity and Culture*

PHILIP GRAHAM RYKEN

P&R
PUBLISHING
P.O. BOX 817 • PHILLIPSBURG • NEW JERSEY 08865-0817

Unless otherwise indicated, Scripture quotations are from the HOLY BIBLE, NEW INTERNATIONAL VERSION®. NIV®. Copyright © 1973, 1978, 1984 by International Bible Society. Used by permission of Zondervan Publishing House. All rights reserved.

Scripture quotations marked NKJV are from The Holy Bible, New King James Version. Copyright © 1979, 1980, 1982, Thomas Nelson, Inc.

Scripture quotations marked KJV are from the King James Version of the Bible.

Scripture quotations marked ESV are from The Holy Bible, English Standard Version, copyright © 2001 by Crossway Bibles, a division of Good News Publishers. Used by permission. All rights reserved.

*Page design by Kirk DouPonce, Dog Eared Design*
*Typesetting by Lakeside Design Plus*

Printed in the United States of America

**Library of Congress Cataloging-in-Publication Data**

Ryken, Philip Graham, 1966–
    He speaks to me everywhere : meditations on Christianity and culture / Philip Graham Ryken.
        p. cm.
    Includes bibliographical references and indexes.
    ISBN 0-87552-797-3
    1. Presbyterian Church in America—Sermons. 2. Sermons, American. I. Title.

BX9178.R95H4 2004
252'.05136—dc22

                                                        2004051003

To

Mark Amstutz, Beatrice Batson, Joe Bean,
Lyle Dorsett, Arthur Holmes,
Bruce Howard, Kathleen Kastner, Lyman Kellstedt, Roger Lundin,
Mark Noll, Leland Ryken, Joe Spradley, John Walford,
Robert Webber, Jay Wood,
and the other outstanding Wheaton College faculty
who taught me the Christian worldview

*Christo et Regno Ejus*
For Christ and His Kingdom

# CONTENTS

**Part Eight    Church History**

**Part Nine    Christianity Today**

# FOREWORD

We often hear that Christianity—especially Christianity shaped by the Reformation—relates to all of life. *All of life?* Would that include e-mail? DNA? T-Ball? Sleep? April Fool's Day? A pig on an airplane?

All of these topics are treated here by Philip Ryken, pastor of Tenth Presbyterian Church in Philadelphia, who turns them into meditations on living the Christian life in a culture that has forgotten God, even though he rules just the same.

They also show a pastor at work, teaching and leading his flock through the issues of the contemporary life. Every Sunday evening, he talks about some current issue, presenting it through a biblical lens. These "Windows on the World" are printed here.

Though many people today think the world is meaningless, the biblical worldview makes all kinds of connections. The Brooklyn Dodgers and the Third Use of the Law. A mother's womb and the Tabernacle. The Theology of Humor. These meditations show that theology is not an abstruse, academic specialty, a matter of lofty abstractions. Rather, theology, in all of its doctrinal rigor, illuminates everything it touches. As Pastor Ryken says, "I am interested in almost everything, and theology is *about* everything."

These meditations also demonstrate just how vast, rich, and comprehensive is the biblical worldview. The Christian account is so much *bigger* than the human ideologies that presume to compete against it. Here are treatments of work *and* leisure, the individual *and* society, mothers *and* fathers, the present *and* the past, seriousness *and* fun.

The Christian view here is set against false religions, liberal judges, and scientific materialists. Their positions are so simplistic, so narrow, so small, compared to the scope and the breadth of biblical truth.

We see how the Islamic insistence that women cover themselves up with the *burqa* not only mistreats women but violates humanity itself, since in our need for human relationships we must see each other face to face. We see how the false theologies currently in vogue—even among those who think they are "evangelical"—pale in the face of historic Christian orthodoxy.

We also see a model of pastoral care. We see Pastor Ryken helping his congregation work their way through the horror of the September 11 attacks and their aftermath, balancing the need for justice *and* the need for forgiveness, affirming our nation while upholding the greater providence of God. He helps them face up to the scandal of racial division in the church. He walks his congregation through milestones of church history (beginning not just with the Church Fathers but with the Church Mothers), teaching his people the rich heritage they have as Christians. Then there are the "big issues" Christians must deal with today—abortion, homosexuality, and other evils that our current culture somehow thinks are good—which he treats with both firmness and pastoral sensitivity.

This is exactly what we laypeople need from our pastors, practical help in walking through the mine fields of contemporary life and in developing a biblical perspective on all of life.

Gene Edward Veith, Ph.D.
Cultural Editor, *World Magazine*

# INTRODUCTION

*Christianity includes all of life. Every realm of knowledge,
every aspect of life and every fact of the universe find their place
and their answer within Christianity.*

FRANK GAEBELEIN

Many people have a deep sense of unease about where our culture is going. The titles of recent books by experienced observers hardly give us much reason for optimism: *Amusing Ourselves to Death* (Neil Postman); *The Twilight of American Culture* (Morris Berman); *The Culture of Disbelief* (Stephen Carter); *Slouching Towards Gomorrah* (Robert Bork). What is the problem? Why do thoughtful people think we are heading for disaster?

Different analysts answer this question in different ways. Some blame the structures of modern media and the way they feed our insatiable appetite for entertainment. Others point to the way radical individualism threatens the stability of our legal, political, social, and educational institutions. Still others blame pluralism and its misguided demand for absolute tolerance. Modernism, postmodernism—call it what you will—there are many disturbing trends in contemporary culture.

One of the more troubling aspects of the current situation is directly related to the theme of this book, namely, the absence of a unified perspective on the world that brings coherence to public life. Western culture does not have a worldview, at least not a consistent one. A worldview is a set of basic ideas about the universe that guide human thought and conduct. Yet today one would be hard pressed to identify any coherent set of ideas that fosters a sense of community and purpose in contemporary culture. Instead, we are confronted with a dizzying kaleidoscope of incoherent commitments.

The Walt Disney Concert Hall in Los Angeles is a symbol of our cultural disarray. The building, which was designed by the renowned architect Frank Gehry and completed in October of 2003, is home to the Los Angeles Philharmonic and other artistic institutions. Its startling façade consists of huge, curving panels of stainless steel that are juxtaposed at chaotic angles. The Concert Hall seems to be moving in different directions at once, which is an apt metaphor for our times: things are coming apart.

At first it might appear that this book is part of the problem. A quick glance through the Table of Contents shows that it covers a wide range of topics, only loosely grouped into general categories. There is a reason for this apparent lack of organization: the chapters in this book were first delivered as occasional talks at Tenth Presbyterian Church in Philadelphia. Since joining the church's pastoral staff in 1995, I have given Sunday evening talks in a series called "Window on the World." Each week I discuss something that is happening in the world from the biblical point of view. (With the exception of the summer and the third Sunday of each month when we have our evening communion service, these talks are posted weekly on the Tenth Church website: www.tenth.org.)

The world is a complicated place, so like the original talks, this book addresses a wide variety of issues. However, there is a coherent perspective that unifies the book and runs through all its chapters. This perspective is the Christian worldview, and its basic principles include the following:

- *Creation:* God made the world and everything in it
- *The Image of God:* men, women, and children are made in the likeness of God

- *Law:* God has revealed one standard of righteousness for all people
- *Sin:* in our rebellion we have broken God's law, and now the whole world is corrupted by sin
- *Salvation:* God is working to rescue his people and renew his creation through the death and resurrection of Jesus Christ
- *Providence:* by the wise counsel of his will, God governs and sustains the world that he has made
- *The Lordship of Christ:* in all of life Jesus rules over the people he is working to save
- *Final Judgment:* the world will end when Jesus Christ returns to punish the wicked and take his people into everlasting joy
- *The Glory of God:* the goal of all things is for God to be praised

One further principle of the Christian worldview deserves special mention: the doctrine of common grace. Theologians make a distinction between the grace God shows his people in salvation (saving grace) and the grace he shows to humanity in general (common grace). God has not reserved all his gifts for Christians. Even the ungodly are graced by his goodness, for "the LORD is good to all, and his mercy is over all that he has made" (Ps. 145:9 ESV). This is God's common grace—common in the sense that it belongs to everyone as part of our common life in this world.

Common grace is not saving grace. In the words of the systematic theologian Louis Berkhof, it "does not pardon or purify human nature, and does not effect the salvation of sinners." Nevertheless, there is something gracious about it, and thus it has a positive influence on the world. As Berkhof goes on to say, common grace "curbs the destructive power of sin, maintains in a measure the moral order of the universe, thus making an orderly life possible, distributes in varying degrees gifts and talents among men, promotes the development of science and art and showers untold blessings upon the children of men."[1] In short, common grace includes every divine blessing short of salvation. The lesser gifts of God's common grace should never be confused with the blessings of his saving grace, but they should still be received as gifts from God.

Common grace means that God is concerned about far more than sin and salvation. He takes an active interest in all the life of the world that he has made. God is as concerned about the body as he is the soul, about the state as he is the church, and about public life as he is personal religion. God is concerned about everything, including romance, marriage, sports, science, racism, fashion, terrorism, archaeology, and all the other topics addressed in this book. I have written about all these things because they interest me too. In fact, this is why I am a theologian. I am interested in almost everything, and theology is *about* everything. It is about everything because it is about God, who speaks to us everywhere.

# Part One

# LOVE, MARRIAGE, AND FAMILY

*Human sexuality is either something that has a nature and a telos, an end, or it is an arbitrary human experience suitable for reconfiguring however we want to. If we believed the former and we were trying to understand and evaluate the place of sexuality in social experience, we would proceed to ask whether or not various institutions do justice to promoting sound convictions and encouraging practices that guard and honor the nature of human sexuality.*

KEN MYERS

THE FAMILY IS LIKE THE CANARY down the mineshaft. According to tradition, coal miners would take a canary with them underground for safety. Canaries are fragile birds, and thus they are the first to suffer the harmful effects of unhealthy air. In the event of a lack of oxygen or a sudden influx of noxious gas, the canary would pass out and the miners would know that they needed to return to the surface.

In the same way, the vitality of the family indicates the quality of our cultural atmosphere. Families only flourish when they can draw deeply from virtues like love, commitment, compassion, and sacrifice. Where these things are missing, it is hard for them to breathe.

What is happening to families today? They are not unconscious, perhaps, but they are gasping for spiritual life. The demand for individual autonomy, the pursuit of sexual pleasure, and the lack of respect for other persons have broken the traditional patterns of courtship. When they do manage to get married, husbands and wives are unable to offer one another the kind of sacrifice and submission that make love grow. Parenting is a lost art. Children are pushed to pursue their own ambitions, but they are not trained to give their lives away for others. Then there are all the non-traditional approaches to family life, many of which are intentionally anti-religious.

Christians do a fair amount of hand wringing over all this, which is understandable. The crumbling of the family eventually leads to the collapse of the culture. However, it also gives us an extraordinary opportunity to witness for Christ. Where will people see patterns of courtship that preserve both passion and purity? Where will they see wives live out the joy of submissive love? Where will they see men lay down their lives for their wives and children in servant sacrifice? Where will they see parents teach their children to live for God and his glory?

They will not see these things in a culture where families are fainting from the toxicity of the surrounding spiritual atmosphere. They will only see them in homes where Christ is at the center and his gospel is the air that we breathe.

# 1

# CAMPUS COURTSHIP

There used to be rules for courtship, and the rules went something like this: Boy meets girl. Boy shows obvious interest in girl. Girl carefully expresses possible interest in boy. Boy speaks with girl's father for permission to spend time with girl. If all went well, eventually the boy and the girl would become engaged and get married.

It all sounds very old-fashioned. It also sounds like the girl doesn't have very much say in the matter. Her options are limited, with little opportunity to take the initiative. Therefore, this model of courtship usually is condemned for leaving women powerless. But what happens when there aren't any rules? What happens to women then?

Some answers are provided by a 2001 study from New York City's Institute for American Values. The study, which was written by Elizabeth Marquardt and Norval Glenn, is called "Hooking Up, Hanging Out, and Hoping for Mr. Right: College Women on Dating and Mating Today." Its findings are saddening, if not surprising.

For starters, the study shows that most college women still have a strong desire to get married. More than eighty percent agree that "being married is a very important goal for me," and most would like to meet their future husband in college.

Unfortunately, there is almost a total absence of social norms to provide a relational structure that could actually lead to a healthy marriage. What prevails instead is a "hookup culture," in which students often "get together for a physical encounter and don't necessarily expect anything further." Most of the college women studied admitted that they were left confused by the lack of clear rules regarding intimacy, romance, courtship, and sex. As another group of experts describes the situation, "American men and women have been left pretty much to their devices in the selection of a marriage partner, in the negotiation of a betrothal, and in the timing of marriage."[1] This is a troubling sign that our culture is in serious disarray.

But what about dating? Dating used to play a significant role in the courtship process. However, the Institute for American Values concludes that dating has changed, so that now it has two almost contradictory meanings. Sometimes the term is used as a synonym for "hanging out." College men and women often spend a good deal of loosely organized time together without making their romantic interest in one another explicit. On the other hand, "dating" can also describe a "fast-moving committed relationship that includes sexual activity, sleeping at the partner's dorm room most nights, sharing meals, and more, but rarely going out on 'dates'," in the traditional sense of the word. These intense relationships often end in painful breakups. This is largely because sex has entered the relationship at the wrong place—before marriage rather than after.

Neither of these two kinds of "dating" involves anything like traditional courtship. The resulting confusion makes it hard for a college woman to figure out where she stands. Is the young man she has been seeing committed to her or not? The anxiety builds until finally she initiates "the talk" that clarifies the relationship. But the man is the one who actually decides where the relationship is going. The authors of the study find this confusing, but from the biblical point of view, it is a reminder that in romantic relationships, men are designed to lead.

The authors rightly conclude that the current rules for dating are deeply destructive for women. They write: "If most college women name marriage as an important goal and most say they would like to meet their future husband at college, then we do them no favors by letting them sort out the pathway to marriage almost completely on their own."

I have some pastoral advice about all of this. Courtship and marriage are matters of profound spiritual significance. Therefore, men and women should not try to figure them out on their own. Christians who have romantic interests or who are in some kind of relationship ought to seek spiritual counsel from someone older and wiser, preferably from Christians who are married. And married Christians should be ready and willing to fulfill their God-given role as guides for courtship and romance. This is my first piece of advice: Get (and give) good counsel.

Second, begin to follow the biblical pattern for relationships between men and women. The Bible says nothing at all about dating. Nor does it provide any kind of handbook for courtship. But it does teach that in marriage, men are to exercise spiritual leadership by showing the sacrificial love of Christ, and women are to respond by showing the submissive love of Christ (see Eph. 5:21–33). This has profound implications for courtship because it sets the pattern for a love relationship between a man and a woman.

Single Christian men should take some initiative. They should actively cultivate friendships with single Christian women. (Incidentally, if a woman says that she is not interested, she should be taken at her word. "No" means no, no matter how tactfully it is expressed.) At each stage it is the man's responsibility to clarify the relationship. If it is only a friendship, the man should make that clear. If it is becoming something more, the man should say what he is hoping it will become, and give a woman the chance to decide whether it is a relationship she also wants to pursue. Most of the long and agonizing discussions couples have about their relationship could be avoided entirely, if only men would show a little spiritual leadership.

As the relationship develops, a woman should practice the biblical virtue of submission. If she has to take the lead—and unfortunately, she often feels like she has to—the relationship is unlikely to lead to marriage, at least not a healthy one.

The problem is that most people do not follow the pastoral advice that I have just given. Many Christian men fail to take spiritual initiative in their relationships with women. Sometimes Christian women frustrate the process by failing to respond to what leadership they do show. On the other hand, many Christian women handle their relationships in a godly way and yet wait in vain for someone to love them in a sacrificial way.

All of this produces a great deal of suffering. This should not surprise us. We live in a fallen world, and one of the first things the Fall affected was relationships between men and women. As we struggle with these issues—whether we are married or single, in or out of a relationship—what we all need is the love of Christ. We need his love to show us how to love one another, and to bring healing to all the places where we have been wounded in what sometimes seems like a loveless world.

# 2

# IN PRAISE OF MODESTY

Probably it was inevitable. Sooner or later it was bound to happen. In the year 2000 Haverford College decided to allow its students to share coed rooms.[1] Male and female undergraduates who live in the Haverford College Apartments, which are home to one-third of the student body, are now able to share a bedroom without breaking the rules.

The administration at Haverford gave two reasons for the change. One was to allow students to share a bedroom with their "significant others." The other was to enable homosexual students to room with someone they felt comfortable with. Prior to the change in Haverford's housing policy, gay and lesbian activists had charged college housing officials with "heterosexism."

Haverford was the first institution of higher education in the Philadelphia area to adopt such a liberal housing policy, but it is unlikely to be the last. The trend has been for universities to have coed dorms, then coed floors, coed suites, and finally even coed bathrooms. This probably explains why news of the change did not cause much of a stir on Haverford's campus. Most students were already used to sharing bathrooms and other communal living areas with members of the opposite sex.

Coed cohabitation shows how difficult it is for postmodern Americans to establish clear boundaries. The effect of the policy is to create widespread confusion about what constitutes appropriate intimacy between unmarried men and women. As one woman from Haverford explained, "In this situation we have now, where you're exposed to sharing a bathroom with guys, it's very normal after a year of doing it." Which is exactly the problem. With a little bit of practice, a living situation that ought to be considered highly abnormal becomes an ordinary part of daily life, especially when it is reinforced by television programs like *Real World* and *Friends*.

In the current climate, even Christian students can become confused about moral propriety in male-female relationships. From time to time I encounter college students or recent graduates who are genuinely surprised when I explain that it is inappropriate for single men and women to live together, even in groups, and even if they are not involved with one another romantically.

The obvious reason that coed living arrangements are inappropriate is the danger of sexual sin. Haverford's assumption seems to be that young men and women are so desensitized that they can sleep in close quarters without ever violating appropriate boundaries. Apparently the college takes the view that sin either doesn't happen, or doesn't matter. Yet physical proximity often plays a significant role in sexual temptation. Haverford's director of student housing is aware of this, but claims that most "students are smart enough to know that [living together] is not a good idea." If it's not a good idea, then one wonders why the college allows it! It would be safer to assume that students are *not* smart enough to avoid temptation, and to set campus housing policy accordingly.

What Haverford should have done was to follow the example of Joseph, who ran for his life when he was invited to sleep with his master's wife. Or the advice of the apostle Paul, who warned Timothy to "flee the evil desires of youth" (2 Tim. 2:22), and who told the Thessalonians to "abstain from all appearance of evil" (1 Thess. 5:22 KJV).

Ironically, a lax attitude toward human sexuality makes for bad sex because it inhibits romance, and therefore hinders marriage. If sexual freedom outside of marriage were good for male-female relationships, then one would expect romance to flourish on today's campuses. Quite the opposite is the case. Dating is down, while sexually transmitted diseases, Internet pornography, and eating disorders are all up. In the absence of clear boundaries, college students lack the proper context for their sexuality. Rather than promoting the joys of true intimacy, the prevailing culture of immodesty prevents intimacy by making public what should be kept private.

In a recent essay Daniel P. Moloney argued that the constant barrage of sexual messages on a college campus

> forces the students to detach themselves from their natural inclinations. . . . they tune out the sexual dimension to their surroundings. . . . This survival reflex, though, confuses them when they try to begin a romantic relationship. They . . . engage in oddly disengaged relationships, usually with a significant sexual component. Instead of going on dates, for example, students hang out in each other's rooms; a bit of alcohol in that setting and you have the beginning of the typical relationship. When the new couple fight, they stop sleeping together; when they break up, they still hang out in each other's rooms.[2]

What they cannot do is establish committed, satisfying, long-term, romantically exciting relationships. The problem is not the absence of sexual opportunity, but its overabundance.

One way for a Christian student to thrive in a culture of sexual confusion is to cultivate the virtue of modesty. Modesty is decency or decorum, especially with regard to sexuality. A modest person is careful to think, speak, act, and live in ways that preserve both one's own purity, and the purity of others. Although it is a virtue that both men and women should cultivate, modesty seems especially valuable to women. In a culture that confuses sex for love, women have a particular interest in preserving sexual intimacy for marriage.

Modesty is a Christian virtue because it recognizes the totality of human depravity. One result of the first sin was that Adam and Eve were no longer able to be naked with one another. In fact, the first thing they did after they ate the forbidden fruit was to cover themselves with fig leaves (Gen. 3:7). To this day, the reason we cannot be naked with one another is because we are sinners. Allowing coed dorm rooms is a way of pretending that we can go back to paradise, when in fact we are living east of Eden.

The Bible teaches that "to the pure, all things are pure" (Titus 1:15). I suppose that could even include coed dorm rooms. The trouble is that we are not pure. Instead of pretending that we are, we should cover our impurity with the virtue of modesty.

# 3

# A HUSBAND OF
# NOBLE CHARACTER

My father always liked to read Proverbs 31 on Mother's Day; however, I'm not sure my mother appreciated it. Proverbs 31 is a poem of praise for "The Wife of Noble Character." It was written by King Lemuel, who knew how to lay it on pretty thick:

> A wife of noble character who can find?
>     She is worth far more than rubies. . . .
> She gets up while it is still dark;
>     she provides food for her family
>     and portions for her servant girls.
> She considers a field and buys it;
>     out of her earnings she plants a vineyard.
> She sets about her work vigorously;
>     her arms are strong for her tasks. . . .
> She is clothed with strength and dignity;
>     she can laugh at the days to come.
> She speaks with wisdom,
>     and faithful instruction is on her tongue. . . .
> "Many women do noble things,
>     but you surpass them all." (Prov. 31:10, 15–17, 25–26, 29)

Not many women compare favorably with Lemuel's description, but my mother happens to be one of them. She *is* a noble woman, so it didn't take much imagination for us to see her in Lemuel's song. My father was not trying to be ironic when he read Proverbs 31. But, as I say, my mother felt somewhat differently. Proverbs 31 made her feel guilty, I think, for she knew that she could never fully measure up to the biblical ideal.

On Mother's Day women like my mother deserve a break. Instead of always thinking about the wife of noble character, it is worth considering her husband. It is sometimes said that behind every good man, there stands a good woman. One of the things we learn from Proverbs 31 is that the reverse is also true: behind every noble wife, there stands a godly husband.

King Lemuel tells us at least three things about the noble husband. First, he trusts his wife completely: "Her husband has full confidence in her" (Prov. 31:11a). If this woman is going to do all the things described in this chapter, he is going to need to have full confidence in her. Not only does she do the shopping, but this woman also does the gardening, runs a small business, makes her own clothes, and invests in real estate. She is active in social work, caring for the needs of the poor (Prov. 31:20). She teaches her children everything they need to know (Prov. 31:26). In short, "she watches over the affairs of her household" (Prov. 31:27a).

Now in order for her to do all these things, the wife of noble character must have the complete trust and unconditional support of her husband. If he were always looking over her shoulder, finding fault with her way of doing things, or insisting on doing everything himself, she would never have the freedom to develop her gifts as God intended. But the noble husband depends on his wife to look after the needs of their family.

Second, the man takes care of his own business. He, too, is a hard worker, a man who provides for the needs of his family. He fulfills the calling that God has given him. Lemuel writes, "Her husband is respected at the city gate, where he takes his seat among the elders of the land" (Prov. 31:23). The noble husband has a place of spiritual leadership in the community. And of course the way a man gains that kind of respect is by working hard, building relationships, giving wise counsel, and generally conducting himself with dignity and integrity. One of the things that motivates the wife of noble character is her husband's nobility. She finds her joy in watching over her own household so that her husband can watch over the work of the whole community. She knows that his honor is also her honor.

Finally, the noble husband encourages his wife: "Her children arise and call her blessed; her husband also, and he praises her" (Prov. 31:28). This, too, is absolutely essential. A woman's work is extremely demanding, both at home and in the wider community. It is very hard to persevere in difficult work without getting constant encouragement. If a husband has a critical spirit, his wife will not flourish; she will struggle in her work, and she will never become the woman God wants her to be. But the noble husband recognizes his responsibility to be his wife's number one supporter.

It is worth noticing the basis for his encouragement. He does not praise his wife for her physical beauty. There is a place for that: just read the Song of Songs. But Lemuel was a wise man, and he knew that inner beauty is far more important than outward beauty. So he said, "Charm is deceptive, and beauty is fleeting; but a woman who fears the LORD is to be praised" (Prov. 31:30).

A few years ago, a young bachelor told me that he was looking for a "P-31." I said, "What's that?" He said, "You know, Proverbs 31. That's the kind of woman I'm looking for." I told him he had better start becoming a P-31 himself—a man of noble character. I had two reasons. First, a woman who comes anywhere close to Proverbs 31 will be looking for the same kind of husband. Second, a wife does not become noble all at once. Proverbs 31 is the work of a lifetime, and it requires the kind of husband who is also described in the passage.

So I ask husbands, Is your wife the kind of woman King Lemuel had in mind? Hopefully, by the grace of God, she is at least starting to become a woman of noble character. But understand that what kind of wife she becomes generally depends on what kind of husband she has.

# 4

## KEEP YOUR EYE ON THE DAD

Fatherhood is a dying institution in America. Some of the reasons for this are explored in a book called *Fatherless America*.[1] At the beginning, author David Blankenhorn defines the current crisis:

> The United States is becoming an increasingly fatherless society. A generation ago, an American child could reasonably expect to grow up with his or her father. Today, an American child can reasonably expect not to. . . . Tonight, about 40 percent of American children will go to sleep in homes in which their fathers do not live. . . . Never before have so many children grown up without knowing what it means to have a father."[2]

Blankenhorn goes on to call fatherlessness "the engine driving our most urgent social problems."

But *Fatherless America* does more than define the problem. It also tries to define what it means to be a good father. Among other things, Blankenhorn argues that simply having a father at home helps bring stability to a child's life. This is not only good sociology; it is also good theology. The Bible begs fathers to turn their hearts back home (Mal. 4:6).

A father who remains committed to his wife and his children brings blessing to his family and his nation.

But it is not easy to be a good father. Every week I have questions that are hard (or even impossible) to answer. How do I parcel out my affection equally among my children? How should I handle a noisy two-year-old during family devotions? What is the most effective means of discipline for a particular act of disobedience? How can I encourage my children to excel without burdening them with unreasonable expectations?

I think about that last question especially during the T-Ball season. You learn a lot about family dynamics when you play T-Ball. I have a great deal of respect for most of the dads in our league. They take an interest in their children. They help with baseball practice. They show up for games. But I have also observed that some fathers have trouble knowing how to handle their children's failures. They get frustrated over simple mistakes. And since what happens on the baseball field is beyond their control, sometimes they even get angry. And this is only T-Ball . . . just wait until we start keeping score!

What some of us end up doing is exactly what the Bible tells us not to do, namely, exasperating our children (see Eph. 6:4). What could be more exasperating than being held to a standard it is impossible to meet, and then being criticized for not meeting it?

What makes unreasonable demands so exasperating is that children need the approval of their fathers. And rightly so! By biblical definition, a father is a man who "has compassion on his children" (Ps. 103:13). Children crave the constant affection of their fathers.

I was reminded of my own son's need for approval by two incidents during his first baseball season. For most of the spring, he did not have much trouble hitting a baseball. But during one memorable at-bat, he repeatedly hit the tee instead of the ball. And it was obvious what his problem was. He was not keeping his eye on the ball; he was looking right at me instead. He was unable to get a base hit until finally I stepped out of sight.

Later, we had a good talk about it. "Do you know why you kept missing the ball?" I asked.

"I don't know. I just kept missing it."

"Well, where were you looking?"

"I don't know."

"I'll tell you where you were looking. You weren't looking at the ball, you were looking at me! Is that what the coach taught you to do: 'Keep your eye on the dad'?" We made a joke about that the rest of the season. "All right, buddy, keep your eye on the dad!" I would say. Then we'd both laugh.

What the incident shows is the power of fatherly approval. My son wanted me to take pleasure in his accomplishment even before he accomplished it. I observed the same desire at work the time he caught a pop fly. Before he threw the ball over to first base to complete the double-play, he glanced over his shoulder to make sure I had seen his catch.

In a way, I am touched that my son wants me to take pleasure in his success. But I am also awestruck by my responsibility as a father. A father's love means almost everything to a child. It establishes his or her identity. It brings peace, security, and joy. If a father's affection matters so much, then it had better be easy to win. It had better be the kind of affection that is just as strong after a strikeout as it is after a grand slam.

The wonderful thing is that constant affection is exactly what every child of God receives from his or her heavenly Father. The prophet Zephaniah described it like this:

> The LORD your God . . . will take great delight in you,
> he will quiet you with his love,
> he will rejoice over you with singing. (Zeph. 3:17)

Every child of God enjoys the irresistible, unbreakable approval of God the Father. If you have received the Father's love through Jesus Christ, then you should keep your on the Dad after all.

# 5

# A MOTHER'S TOUCH

Almost everyone in America has heard of Theodore Kaczynski: graduate of Harvard, teacher of mathematics, despiser of technology, resident of Montana, maker of terrorist threats, and designer of bombs, or should that be "Unabombs"? There is little doubt that Kaczynski is an odd fellow, ill-suited for life in the twenty-first century.

As is always the case when disaster strikes, journalists scramble for answers. The secular mind is never satisfied with attributing evil to total depravity. Some further explanation or rationalization for human sin is always needed.

In Kaczynski's case, there were no shortage of explanations for his strangeness. One report, especially, caught my attention:

> Investigators say that at the age of six months [Kaczynski] was hospitalized for several weeks after suffering an allergic reaction to a drug. During that time, his parents were not allowed to hold or hug him. When he came home, they found him listless and withdrawn. In light of that early denial of human contact, investigators are intrigued by the fact that one of the Unabomber's early targets was James McConnell, a professor of psychology at the University of Michigan who eventually became well known for research into the benefits of

sensory deprivation for autistic children. Investigators were told that in childhood Ted seemed to avoid human contact.[1]

That is a haunting report. It gives us a pitiable picture of a young boy isolated from his mother and cut off from society. It confirms the sad truth of the biblical proverb "A child left to himself disgraces his mother" (Prov. 29:15b). Kaczynski's abandonment may well have had something to do with his subsequent inability to develop healthy relationships with women or to find his place in human society. It is impossible to underestimate the value of a mother's touch. An infant cannot thrive without it. Nothing else in the whole world can compare with it.

Dorothy Kunhardt's book *Pat the Bunny* invites children to interact by patting a soft bunny, or looking into a mirror, or putting a finger through "Mommy's ring."[2] One page says this: "Judy can feel Daddy's scratchy face. Now YOU feel Daddy's scratchy face." The man on the page has sandpaper whiskers on his cheek that a child can actually touch. A father's cheek can be imitated. But not a mother's cheek. What substance could one put in a book to simulate a mother's touch?

At our house, we have two flavors of parent. Lisa comes in a different parental flavor than I do. She is soft where I am scratchy, gentle where I am rough, flexible where I am unyielding. There are times when our oldest son prefers my flavor, like when it's time to play football. But other times he prefers Lisa's flavor, like when he gets hurt playing football, just to name one. Having two flavors of parent to choose from is a gift from God.

There may be a danger in exaggerating the differences between mothers and fathers. Mothers, like fathers, are to be strong in discipline and in training their children to be independent. Fathers, like mothers, are to be gentle and tender with their sons and daughters. But surely God intends mothers to be, well, motherly. In fact, whenever we see mothers act in a maternal way, we catch a glimpse of the character of God. The Lord says to his people: "As a mother comforts her child, so will I comfort you" (Isa. 66:13). This verse needs no explanation. We have seen mothers comfort their children, and most of us can still remember what it feels like to *be* comforted by our mothers. To see ourselves as children on God's lap gives us hope that all our hurts will be healed.

But even if Isaiah's promise needs no explanation, it needs plenty of *application*. We need to see mothers touch like mothers in order to understand the comfort of God. Some mothers may feel unequal to the task of motherhood. Mothers realize how far short they fall of the biblical ideal. But they should be encouraged that even the simplest tasks of mothering—like touching the forehead of a sick child—are a powerful demonstration of the love of God.

Women who are not mothers should also be encouraged. They have the same touch. It is a hard thing for a woman with strong maternal instincts to go through life without experiencing the so-called "Joys of Motherhood." Even though we are not naïve about the burdens and sorrows of motherhood, we recognize that motherhood *is* a gift from God. So women who remain unmarried or are unable to bear children may have feelings of loss or disappointment about not becoming mothers.

But remember that the church is your family. If you have a desire to nurture children, then your maternal impulse is welcome in the family of God. You can be a blessing to the children in God's family, as all of us share together in the responsibility of caring for the children of the church.

# 6

# DOMESTIC PARTNERS

A recent lawsuit has significant implications for the institution of marriage in Philadelphia. The story begins in May of 1998, when then-Philadelphia mayor Ed Rendell signed into law a city ordinance creating a new marital status called a "Life Partnership." This term referred to any long-term relationship between adults of the same gender, also known as "domestic partners." The effect of the mayor's decree was to extend "health care and leave benefits to the domestic partners of all non-civil service City employees." In other words, the city would cover live-in partners of homosexual employees as if they were married.

Later that year Bill Devlin of the Urban Family Council filed a lawsuit against the city, claiming that Philadelphia had unlawfully attempted to redefine the institution of marriage. Devlin and other litigants lost their case two years later, when the Common Pleas Court upheld the city's "Life Partnership" ordinance. But later the Commonwealth Court of Pennsylvania overruled, declaring that only the state and not the local government has the right to define marriage. To quote from the court's opinion, "The City did indeed act beyond the scope of its power . . . when it defined and created for legal purposes a new relationship between same-sex persons that it categorized as being part and parcel of the marital status."

As of this writing, the case is not yet over, because Mayor John Street appealed to the Pennsylvania Supreme Court. This was not unexpected, but it marked a major change of opinion for the mayor. Back in 1996, when the legislation was first proposed, then-Council President Street said, "I believe the Domestic Partnership Executive Order constitutes a lessening of the city's support for the institution of marriage, and that it represents a 'frontal assault' on our City's families; in my opinion, this executive order circumvents the legislative process and subverts the will of the majority of the members of City Council, and the people they represent."[1] Later Mayor Street changed his mind and acted to support the law he once opposed.

What was curious about the city's ordinance was that it only applied to homosexual partners, and not to people who were living together in other so-called committed relationships. Why did the city extend benefits to gay and lesbian partners but not to other live-in boyfriends and girlfriends? What was the reason for this inconsistency? Simply this: the ordinance was an attempt to legitimize homosexual behavior by granting it the status and benefits of marriage.

At present there is nothing to prevent unmarried persons—of whatever gender or sexual orientation—from living together. Couples can set up housekeeping, share income and expenses, engage in sexual intercourse, and raise children without ever getting married. But as Gregory Koukl has explained, "What such couples don't enjoy is respect. Marriage is society's way of welcoming a couple into the community, declaring the union honorable and legitimate. It's the community's official stamp of support and approval."[2]

This explains why some members of the gay community have been so active in seeking to gain the privileges of marriage: they are trying to legitimize homosexual behavior. For all the stress that marriage is under, it is still one of America's most venerable institutions. It has not yet been robbed of all its dignity, but remains a last bastion of polite society. Thus the gay community views marriage as a goal for gaining communal credibility.

The question is, What constitutes a marriage? And who decides? According to the Bible, marriage is not merely a human convention that we are free to define and redefine, but a divinely ordained covenant. In the opening pages of Scripture it is defined as a loving bond between one man and one woman for life: "For this reason a man will leave his father and mother and be united to his wife, and they will become one flesh" (Gen. 2:24; cf. Mal. 2:14–15). According to God, there is something complementary about marriage. It is the union of the male and the female, which by definition rules out other arrangements.

This biblical definition of marriage clearly forms the basis for Pennsylvania law, which states "that marriage shall be between one man and one woman," and that "a marriage between persons of the same sex . . . shall be void in this Commonwealth."[3] There are good reasons for the state to grant marriage this kind of legal standing, and also to give married couples certain economic advantages. Strong marriages further the common good. They encourage people to work together. They provide the best and safest context for raising children. Thus the government supports marriage as a way of securing the future of a healthy society.

Christians should support marriage, too, and sometimes this means defending it from getting redefined. However, as we defend marriage, we need to be careful how we treat those who are attacking it. This is important to emphasize because Christians sometimes get the idea that since sexual immorality is a sin, it's okay to treat practicing homosexuals like second-class citizens, or even worse, to treat them with contempt. This is not the way of Christ, who calls us to love our neighbors. As followers of Jesus Christ, we are called to defend the basic human and civic rights of all citizens, including practicing homosexuals. We should oppose anything that makes homosexuality the object of ridicule, hatred, or violence.

Having said that, it also needs to be said that as Christians we are not obliged to endorse homosexuality as a lifestyle, which is what the domestic partners debate is really about. We believe that the Bible condemns sexual activity outside the bonds of marriage. This is not some kind of bigotry; it is simply the application of a biblical ethic for human sexuality. Nor is it some kind of discrimination: the joy of sex is offered to anyone and everyone who accepts the obligations of marriage. What we are not free to do is to use sex for our own purposes. Like any other gift from God, it only glorifies him when we use it the way that he intended.

# Part Two

# SPORTS AND LEISURE

*God created people with the capacity and need for rest and leisure. He gave commands that obligate people to set a boundary to their work and the other responsibilities of life. In short, if God calls people to rest, they have an obligation to respond to that calling, just as much as they respond to their calling to work.*

LELAND RYKEN

IT IS FAIRLY WELL KNOWN that Christianity has a theology of work. People still talk about "the Protestant work ethic," for example, or debate the role of good works in salvation.

What are the fundamental principles of a true Christian theology of work? The Bible teaches that we are made in the image of a working God, who tells us, "Whatever you do, work at it with all your heart, as working for the Lord, not for men" (Col. 3:23). Every Christian has a calling—a primary vocation that affords an opportunity to do some-

41

thing useful in the world, and to do it for the glory of God. We do not work to win our way back to God, but as a grateful response to his grace.

What is perhaps less widely known is that Christianity also has a theology of play. The same God who gives us a vocation also governs our avocations.

The Christian theology of play begins with the Sabbath: "By the seventh day God had finished the work he had been doing; so on the seventh day he rested from all his work. And God blessed the seventh day and made it holy, because on it he rested from all the work of creating that he had done" (Gen. 2:2–3). God did the work of making the world in six days, but on the seventh day he took his ease. This then becomes the pattern for our own work and rest: six days of labor and one day of leisure.

God has established this weekly pattern because he is concerned for us as whole persons. We were made to work, but if all we ever did was work, we would soon be exhausted. Thus there is an important place in the Christian life for rest and recreation.

The problem is that like all good things, leisure can easily become an object of idolatry. Few cultures have ever been as obsessed with entertainment as our own: sports, movies, video games, even recreational shopping—the list goes on and on. Everybody seems to be working for the weekend. The most important thing is to have fun, and work is just a necessary means to that end. As has often been observed, Americans tend to play at their work and work at their play.

For the Christian, both work and play come under the lordship of Jesus Christ. As the following essays try to show, we are called to rest as well as to work to the glory of God. This means observing a proper balance between the two in our daily and weekly schedule. It also means keeping God at the center of both labor and leisure. When we pursue his pleasure we find real rest and refreshment in him.

# 7

# THE GOSPEL ACCORDING TO THE OLYMPICS

The Olympic Games are big at the Ryken household, especially the Winter Olympics. Figure skating, ice hockey, bobsled, Super G: we love them all—even curling. We also enjoy the opening and closing ceremonies. The pageantry of the Winter 2002 Olympics was spectacular. There were figure skaters with fireworks, beautiful puppets of Western animals, giant snowballs bouncing around the stadium, a fantasy locomotive, and almost everything else anyone could imagine. Salt Lake City put on a show.

One of the striking features of the 2002 ceremonies was how much use they made of the symbol of light. Light has always been a traditional symbol of the Olympic movement. Before the Games begin, the Olympic torch is carried person-to-person from city to city. In this way an eternal flame is kept burning from one Olympics to the next. Then, while the Games are open, a huge cauldron of fire burns atop the Olympic stadium.

The 2002 Olympic theme had to do with light: "Light the Fire Within." In keeping with this theme, the focal character of the opening and closing ceremonies was a young boy holding out a lantern. He was accompanied by thousands of other young people called "the children of light." Both ceremonies made effective use of light and darkness to convey the power of the light.

What is significant about these symbols of light is that they reflect the Christian Gospel. Jesus Christ is "the light of the world" (John 8:12), the eternal flame, "the true light that gives light to every man" (John 1:9). Everyone who believes in Jesus comes into his light. God lights a fire within, making "his light shine in our hearts to give us the light of the knowledge of the glory of God" (2 Cor. 4:6). That fire within comes from the Holy Spirit, who burns in the mind and heart of every believer. The Spirit's inward illuminating work gives us a special identity. As Jesus said, "Believe in the light, that ye may be the children of light" (John 12:36 KJV).

Light imagery plays all over the pages of the New Testament. And, whether it was deliberate or not, the 2002 Winter Olympics borrowed some of that imagery, trying to capitalize on light's inherent spiritual power. As I watched the light dance across the television screen, it occurred to me how hard the Olympics try to be a spiritual experience. Sometimes they almost promise to solve the problems of the world.

The Olympics are a great force for good. They celebrate the strength, beauty, and agility of the human body. They revel in the vitality of youth. But the most amazing thing about them is the way they bring people together. There is something exciting about seeing nations from all over the world come together for a common purpose. One of the explicit goals of the "Olympic movement," as it is called, is world peace.

On what basis do the Olympics seek to establish this peace? In Salt Lake City there were speeches about the human spirit, about setting aside our differences and coming together. There was also plenty of light, as if the light itself had the power to make things new. Then at the closing ceremonies there was a song that offered a prayer for grace. The Olympics tried to give us peace, unity, light, and grace. But in the end, all they really offered was sports. That's all. Just sports.

Sports are wonderful. Some of my best experiences in life have involved practicing, playing, and coaching sports. In my own personal opinion, there will be sports in heaven. I say this in part because my first eschatological experience—my first foretaste of heaven—took place during a backyard baseball game when I was five years old.

However, sports can only take the world so far, and some of their limitations became obvious during the 2002 Winter Olympics. Sports make some people champions, but they also produce a lot of losers, including sore ones. Sports can lead to bitter disputes and angry disagreements. Sometimes instead of bringing nations together, they drive them apart. And they are subject to all the vagaries of human judgment. Just ask the Korean speed skaters who were disqualified or the woman from France who came under attack for the scores she gave in pairs figure skating. Then there were the cheaters, as there always are.

After all the medals were awarded and all the cheering died down, we discovered that although sports can be an enjoyable hobby, they make a poor religion. They do not shine with true light and they cannot provide a lasting peace. One of the problems with the Olympics is that they don't last forever. After burning brightly for two weeks, the flame over Salt Lake City was extinguished. The light was swallowed in darkness. The Games came to an end, as they always do, and even while the athletes partied on, the feelings of sadness and loss were palpable.

Everything that is good and true about the Olympics points us to what God has given us in Jesus Christ. He is the true light, and one day all nations will gather in his brightness. The Bible promises that when the world and all its games are over, there will be a celebration to end all celebrations. It will be the most amazing spectacle that anyone has ever seen. It will "not need the sun or the moon to shine on it, for the glory of God gives it light, and the Lamb is its lamp. The nations will walk by its light. . . . The glory and honor of the nations will be brought into it" (Rev. 21:23–24, 26).

In that parade of nations there will be no losers, only winners—champions for Christ. Everyone there will be a child of light. And the celebration will last forever.

## 8

# THE TEAM THAT
# DIDN'T HAVE A PRAYER

High school football under the Friday-night lights is a great Texas tradition. However, now something is missing from the pre-game routine. As a result of the Supreme Court decision in *Santa Fe Independent School District v. Doe*, students are no longer allowed to offer public prayers before football games. Formerly, the school district had allowed students to elect a representative to offer an invocation over the loudspeaker before every home game, praying for safety and sportsmanship. But now traditional pre-game prayers are banned.

Predictably, the Supreme Court decision appealed to the so-called "separation of church and state." By a majority of 6–3, the justices ruled that student-led, student-initiated public prayer before a sporting event is not protected by the First Amendment of the Constitution. On the contrary, such prayer is unconstitutional because it represents the establishment of religion.

Writing for the Court, Justice John Paul Stevens argued that,

> school sponsorship of a religious message is impermissible because it
> sends the ancillary message to members of the audience who are non-
> adherents that they are outsiders, not full members of the political

community, and an accompanying message to adherents that they are insiders, favored members of the political community. The delivery of such a message—over the school's public address system by a speaker representing the student body, under the supervision of school faculty and pursuant to a school policy that explicitly and implicitly encourages public prayer—is not properly characterized as "private" speech.

Stevens also claimed that "the religious liberty protected by the Constitution is abridged when the state affirmatively sponsors the particular religious practice of prayer."

The ban on pre-game prayer was the latest and strongest in a long line of Supreme Court decisions opposing prayer in the public schools. It prompted a blitz of protest all over the South. In Forest City, North Carolina, football fans brought portable radios to tune in to a prayer broadcast just before kickoff. In Hattiesburg, Mississippi, a few students in the bleachers began to say "Our Father who art in Heaven," and by the time they were finished, more than 4,000 fans were reciting the Lord's Prayer. In Knoxville, Tennessee, the local chapter of the Fellowship of Christian Athletes formed a human prayer chain on the track surrounding a football field. In Asheville, North Carolina, a rally sponsored by the group "We Still Pray" filled a stadium with 12,000 supporters. And fans at Arkansas' Yellville-Summit High emptied the stands and rushed to the 50-yard line, where they knelt to pray with their cheerleaders.

It is not surprising that so many students have tried to make an end-run around the Supreme Court. For one thing, two out of three Americans think the Court judged incorrectly. For another thing, the decision in *Santa Fe* is a blatant attack on Christianity. In his dissent—in which he argued that the Supreme Court had once again fumbled the relationship between church and state—Chief Justice William Rehnquist warned that the majority opinion "bristles with hostility to all things religious in public life." And so it does. When even something as innocuous as praying before a football game is declared illegal, it cannot be long before Christians will face more severe deprivations. It appears likely that in the future the *Santa Fe* decision will be used to eliminate other forms of prayer, such as the invocations offered at many public school graduations.

It is easy to understand why the Supreme Court ban has angered so many Christians. It is also easy to admire the courage and creativity of those who have found ways to circumvent it. Nevertheless, it is worth asking whether it is wise to use pre-game prayer as a political football. One problem with the recent rash of civil disobedience is that it turns prayer into a form of political protest. This is not entirely the church's fault. After all, it was the Supreme Court that first politicized the issue by ruling that pre-game prayer was an abuse of political power. But Christians should resist the temptation to treat everything as a matter of politics. Prayer is the most powerful weapon in our arsenal, but it is not a political weapon. Instead, God uses it to advance his spiritual kingdom.

Another problem with the pre-game prayer is that it turns prayer into a public spectacle. It is not wrong to pray in public, of course. The Bible encourages us to "pray in the Spirit on all occasions with all kinds of prayers" (Eph. 6:18). It also urges "requests, prayers, intercession and thanksgiving to be made for everyone" (1 Tim. 2:1), including high-school football players. However, there may be times when it is inappropriate to pray out loud and in public. Jesus placed his emphasis on private prayer. "And when you pray," he said, "do not be like the hypocrites, for they love to pray standing in the synagogues and on the street corners to be seen by men. . . . But when you pray, go into your room, close the door and pray to your Father, who is unseen" (Matt. 6:5–6).

Jesus emphasized private intercession because he understood how easy it is for prayer to lead to hypocrisy, especially when it is offered to make someone else take notice. I am reminded of the college student who was trying to convert his roommate to Christianity. When he heard him coming back from a late-night party, he would hop out of bed and say his prayers—kneeling in the middle of the room so his roommate would trip over him in the dark!

True prayer is never offered to get in someone's way, or to make a political point, but to enter the presence of God with praises and petitions. If God is our true audience, we will not find it necessary to pray at the fifty-yard line. And if he has ceased to be our audience, we have ceased truly to pray.[1]

# 9

# THEY CALL ME "COACH"

The best thing about the approach of spring is the start of the baseball season. The worst thing about it is the end of the basketball season. I didn't realize how sad this would be until one day I stood in a locker room and watched an athlete bawl his eyes out because his high school career was over. To put this in context, I should mention that for several years I helped coach the boys basketball team at City Center Academy (CCA).

It was sad to see each season come to an end, even though we ended up with a losing record. There would be no more van trips to road games, no more foul trouble, no more bad calls, no more gut-wrenching losses, no more three-on-two, two-on-one drills, no more practice-ending sprints, no more three-pointers, and no more victories won on last–second shots. The season was over.

Though sad, the end of a season is always a good time to reflect on the lessons we have learned. Basketball is a microcosm of life, and the basketball court is a good place to learn important life lessons, including spiritual lessons.

During the 1998 season our team learned the truth of something I am forever telling my children: "Work first, then play." This is one of the implications of what God says in his Word: "There is a time for everything, and a season for every activity under heaven" (Eccles. 3:1).

Both work and play have their proper times, provided they come in the proper order.

Some of the guys on the team wanted to play without doing all of their schoolwork. As a result, one of our biggest problems was maintaining a full squad. We started the season with fifteen players. At the end of the first marking period I asked the head coach if we had lost anyone because of low grades. "Let me put it this way," he said, "it would be easier to tell you who we've got left!"

The curriculum at CCA is intended to prepare urban high school students for college. Athletes have to maintain at least a "C" average to remain eligible for sports. That is no way to run a winning basketball program, I can assure you, but it is a terrific way to teach self-discipline. There is a time for play, but it comes after all required work has been well done.

Another thing we learned was the importance of listening to the coach. Some of our freshmen were playing organized basketball for the first time. They needed instruction in the fundamentals: stay between your man and the basket, don't pick up your dribble, look at the basket while you are shooting, and so forth. Players who listen to the coach—as nearly all our players did—make progress every week. Players who don't listen drive their coaches to distraction.

Sometimes it is hard to hear the coach, like during the fourth quarter of a close game in front of a noisy crowd. When there are two defenders on you and the entire student body is cheering, it is hard to think straight, let alone listen. But the smart players always have one ear tuned to the bench.

One way to teach players to listen for the coach's voice is not to use a whistle during practice. I learned this from the example of Mike Krzyzewski, who coaches basketball at Duke University. Coach K, as he is called, wants his players to learn how to recognize his voice as soon as he shouts an instruction.

It occurs to me that this is good counsel for the Christian life. Jesus says, "The sheep listen to [the Good Shepherd's] voice. He calls his own sheep by name and leads them out. . . . his sheep follow him because they know his voice" (John 10:3–4). If we are God's sheep then we recognize his voice. But we need to learn how to listen for it so we can follow him. This is not always easy to do, especially when so many other things clamor for our attention: work, family, ministry, pleasure. Unless we are listening for it, we may not hear the Shepherd's voice at all.

A third thing I learned is the value of a servant's heart. Anyone who has ever played on a team knows that not everyone gets to be the star. In fact, some players do not even get to start (unless most of the team is academically ineligible!). However, every player is an important part of the team.

Being a team-player includes helping your teammates any way you can. Sometimes it means filling the water bottles and collecting the basketballs. While coaching, I learned how hard it is to sell aspiring young athletes on the importance of humble service. Like most things of value, servants' hearts are in short supply.

They do exist, however. One of our freshmen showed us a glimpse of one on a road trip early in the season. Unfortunately, one of our key players forgot his jersey, so he was ineligible to play. When the freshman realized how this would hurt the team, he went to the head coach and volunteered to give up his jersey for his teammate.

What would you have done if you had been the coach? On the one hand, learning to take the right equipment is a basic life skill. For most jobs it is necessary to wear the right uniform to work every day. What better way to learn that lesson than to spend one whole basketball game in street clothes?

On the other hand, giving up a jersey was a terrific example of team play. More than that, it was a perfect example of the servant heart of Jesus Christ. It was like a parable of what Jesus did on the cross when he took our sin upon his own back. Now he offers to clothe us in his perfect righteousness. Of all the things I learned during basketball season, this was the best lesson of all.

# 10

# SHOULD I PRAY WHEN I SCORE A TOUCHDOWN?

When are you most likely to see someone pray? Before dinner? During final exams? Shortly before take-off? The answer used to be "in church," but not any more. Prayer is gradually disappearing from Christian worship. Perhaps this is because the invocation of Almighty God is not very "seeker-sensitive."

Maybe the only place you can count on seeing someone pray these days is on Monday Night Football. Football players used to spike the ball when they scored a touchdown. Now they usually get down on one knee to thank God that nobody tackled them. Their teammates still come running down field to celebrate, but first they gather in the end zone for a post-TD prayer meeting.

Should Christians boo or cheer when they see these public displays of religion? Or, to pose the question on everyone's mind: "Should I pray when I score a touchdown?"

On the one hand, prayer is so valuable (not to mention rare) one would hate to do anything to discourage it. Think of Deion Sanders, for example, the flashy cornerback who used to play for the Dallas Cowboys. Deion claimed to have a personal relationship with Jesus Christ, but he admitted that he was not mature in the faith. For instance, he said that he wanted to take a month off to master the Bible, "or how-ever long it takes." Who knows? For some new believers, praying in the end zone may be a significant act of faith.

One suspects, however, that most end zone prayers lack sincerity. As a general rule, professional athletes are a superstitious bunch. So for some of them prayer is just another way to stay lucky. On one occasion, a post-game fight broke out in the Detroit Lions locker room. The fight may have had something to do with the fact that the Lions had just been crushed by the Green Bay Packers, 31-3. But it also had something to do with wide receiver Herman Moore's refusal to join his teammates for post-game prayer. Robert Porcher, the Lions' bad-tempered defensive end, was so upset he tried to sanctify Moore with his fists.

This points out the problem with praying in the end zone and other public places: outward displays of religiosity lead to hypocrisy. That is why Jesus taught his disciples to pray in secret: "And when you pray, do not be like the hypocrites, for they love to pray standing in the syna-gogues and on the street corners to be seen by men. I tell you the truth, they have received their reward in full. But when you pray, go into your room, close the door and pray to your Father, who is unseen. Then your Father, who sees what is done in secret, will reward you" (Matt. 6:5–6). To paraphrase: "Don't be like the football stars who kneel in the corner of the end zone on national TV. But when you pray, go into the locker room and close the door. Then God will answer your prayers."

The other problem athletes face is knowing what to pray for. In the fall of 1996 John Blake was in his first year of coaching for the Univer-sity of Oklahoma Sooners. When Oklahoma upset arch-rival Texas in overtime, Blake was so excited he told ABC-TV, "This was Jesus Christ working through my players." One sportswriter in the New York Times wanted to know where God was the rest of the season, when Oklahoma lost eight games. Did they get outplayed, or just outprayed?

Christian athletes sometimes wonder if they should pray for victory. If so, what happens when players on both teams pray for a win? What if two Christian schools play against each other? Who wins then? It was

President Eisenhower who defined an atheist as "someone who doesn't care who wins the game between Notre Dame and Texas Christian." Part of Eisenhower's point was that Christians are sometimes tempted to intercede for their favorite team.

The cartoonist Doug Marlette often includes religious themes in the comic strip *Kudzu*. One strip depicts two bench-warmers talking theology during a church-league basketball game. Their uniforms indicate that they play for the "Holy Rollers."

"Really, Preacher," one of them says, "if we thank God when we win, shouldn't we *blame* God if we lose? I mean, if He's on our side and he's the Author of all things, then He's doing it—He's making us lose!"

"I see," the pastor dryly observes. "So maybe that's why you missed that game-winning free throw! The Lord willed it!"

"Exactly!" says his teammate. "Don't you love theology?!"

It is true, of course, that divine providence extends to the details of life. In the words of the Westminster Confession, by his providence God "governs all creatures, actions, and things."[1] But God's plan is worked out even through blocks, tackles, fumbles, and everything else that happens on the football field.

I doubt God cares very much who makes the playoffs, which probably means his people should not care too much, either. But it is certain that God cares what happens to the souls of the players who are battling to make the playoffs. So there are plenty of things for Christians who play sports to pray about.

According to the old coaching cliché, "It's not whether you win or lose, but how you play the game." This may not be an attitude that wins many championships, but it is not bad theology. Sports, like every other area of life, provide an arena for godliness. Athletes have daily opportunities to live out the love of Jesus Christ. They should not pray for the kind of success which can be measured in wins and losses. Instead, they should pray that—win or lose—they are faithful to their Head Coach.

## 11

# THE BROOKLYN
# DODGERS AND THE
# THIRD USE OF THE LAW

Back in the early 1940s—a few years before Jackie Robinson became the first African American to play in the major leagues—the Brooklyn Dodgers were managed by Leo "the Lip" Durocher. They called Leo "the Lip" because he was a big mouth. More than once Durocher's comments started a bench-clearing brawl. One of his biographers concluded he was even "too loud and aggressive for the Yankees," so they shipped him to the National League.[1] When he started managing in Brooklyn, the Lip would shout to his pitchers, "Stick it in his ear, stick it in his ear."[2]

One of Durocher's shortcomings was being too hard on young ballplayers. If one of his rookies made an error, "the Lip" would hurl invectives at him from the dugout. By the time the inning was over the youngster had been covered in curses.

Fortunately, the Dodgers had some assistant coaches in those days who had more wisdom and patience. One of them was the kindly Red Corriden. Corriden's job was to restore the rookie's confidence. Back in the dugout, or back in the clubhouse, Red would put his arm around him and speak words of encouragement. He would explain that even

Durocher's verbal abuse was a good sign. It meant that he thought the player had a future in baseball; otherwise, he wouldn't be nearly so upset.

The next day another coach would take over, Charley Dressen, who later went on to lead the Dodgers to the pennant. Dressen would meet the rookie for practice before the next game. He would begin by rehearsing the error he had made the day before. But then he would show the player how to avoid making the same mistake again. Dressen would work with him on his footwork, or his positioning, or his hitting stroke, or on throwing to the proper base.

Why am I telling you all of this? Because the Brooklyn Dodger coaching staff of the 1940s illustrates the use of the law in the Christian life. By "law" I mean the eternal commands of God as they are summarized in the Ten Commandments. Just as the Dodgers had a coach to curse and a coach to teach, so the law of God curses us for our sins and teaches us how to be righteous.

The first thing the law of God does is show us our sin. As soon as we learn that God requires us to love him with all our hearts and to love our neighbors as ourselves, we discover that we are not very good lovers. The law exposes the fact that we love neither God nor our neighbor. As the apostle Paul explained to the Romans, "Through the law we become conscious of sin" (Rom. 3:20). Or again, "I would not have known what sin was except through the law" (Rom. 7:7). Leo Durocher did much the same thing for his Brooklyn Dodgers. He cursed them for their errors.

But the law of God does more than curse. It also drives us to salvation in Jesus Christ. As Augustine observed, "The law bids us, as we try to fulfill its requirements, and become wearied in our weakness under it, to know how to ask the help of grace."[3]

As soon as we know that we are sinners, we see the need to be saved from our sins. We admit that we deserve the eternal wrath of God, we repent of our sins, and we put our faith in Jesus Christ. We run from the law into the arms of our Savior. In his death on the cross we find forgiveness for our lawlessness. And like Red Corriden, Jesus puts his arms around us to tell us everything will be all right.

Once we know Jesus Christ then we have a whole new use for the law. Like Charley Dressen, the law coaches us not to make the same mistakes again. It teaches us how to please God. It shows us how to think and say and do God's will. Now we obey the Ten Commandments, not out of grudging duty, but out of joyful gratitude.

John Calvin called this the "third use of the law." The first use or purpose of the law is to show us our sin. This is where Leo "the Lip" Durocher came in, with all his curses. The second use of the law is to restrain evil. Although the law cannot change the human heart, sometimes it can force us to obey God, especially when God's law becomes the law of the land. As far as I know, the Brooklyn Dodgers didn't have a coach to represent the second use of the law, unless they had someone to collect fines for being late for the train.

The third use or purpose of the law is to teach us how to do good works. Once we know Christ, we are free to "fulfill the law of Christ" (Gal. 6:2; see 1 Cor. 9:21). This use of the law teaches us how to be good Christians, much the way Charley Dressen used to teach young Dodgers how to be good baseball players.

The King James Version of the Bible describes the law as a "schoolmaster to bring us unto Christ" (Gal. 3:24). Having learned about the Brooklyn Dodgers and the third use of the law, we can almost say that the law is also a baseball coach to lead us to Christ. First it curses our sin to show us we need a Savior. But in the end it teaches us how to please the Savior who died for our sins.

# FEELING SLEEPY?

"All work and no sleep makes U.S. a very fatigued nation." Thus read the headline atop an article in the *Philadelphia Inquirer*.[1] It caught my attention because sometimes I feel sleepy myself.

The news story was based on a poll taken by the National Sleep Foundation. The findings were interesting, and in some cases, alarming. Experts say that the average adult needs eight hours of sleep to function effectively. However, two-thirds of Americans get less than that amount, with one-third getting less than seven hours. Compared with numbers from a survey taken five years prior to this one, Americans are sleeping less than ever.

Given these results, it is not surprising that two out of five workers say they have trouble staying awake on the job. In fact, at the same time that Americans are getting less sleep, they are spending more hours on the job. People who work sixty hours a week (or more) usually try to get by on only six hours of sleep a night. For many Americans, sleep deprivation has become a way of life. One spokesperson concluded, "There is an epidemic of sleepiness in our society. Fatigue is widespread. People may be getting sleep, but it is at school, at work and behind the wheel." Obviously, this can be dangerous. Twenty percent of those surveyed admitted that they had actually fallen asleep while driving.

Like everything else in life, sleep is a spiritual issue. On the one hand, the Bible warns against sleeping when there is work to be done. "How long will you lie there, you sluggard? When will you get up from your sleep?" (Prov. 6:9). However, the Bible has nothing good to say about people who spend too much time working and not enough time resting. This is unhealthy, not only physically, but also spiritually and emotionally. The biblical philosopher asked, "What does a man get for all the toil and anxious striving with which he labors under the sun? All his days his work is pain and grief; even at night his mind does not rest. This too is meaningless" (Eccl. 2:22–23). Not only is it meaningless, but it is also useless. The psalmist said, "In vain you rise early and stay up late, toiling for food to eat" (Ps. 127:2).

Sometimes it is impossible to get as much sleep as we need. Personally, I was not surprised to discover that the most sleep-deprived people in America are adults with small children. Even the apostle Paul confessed that on occasion, the difficulties of his missionary work forced him to endure sleepless nights (2 Cor. 6:5).

Nevertheless, God commands us to get enough sleep as often as we can. There are many good reasons for this. For starters, it is hard to work to his glory when we are feeling sleepy. People who are short on their sleep have trouble remembering and concentrating. Studies have even shown that people with poor sleep habits tend to live shorter lives. So it is for our own benefit that God commands us to rest.

This command is found, among other places, in the fifth commandment: "Remember the Sabbath day by keeping it holy. Six days you shall labor and do all your work, but the seventh day is a Sabbath to the LORD your God. On it you shall not do any work, neither you, nor your son or daughter, nor your manservant or maidservant, nor your animals, nor the alien within your gates" (Ex. 20:8–10). This commandment is God's way of helping us remember to get enough rest. It is not intended to be a burden, but a blessing. As Jesus said, "The Sabbath was made for man, not man for the Sabbath" (Mark 2:27). In other words, it is for our own good that God has given us a day of rest.

We find our ultimate rest in the being and work of God. This connection is made in the fifth commandment, where our keeping the Sabbath is based on God's resting from his work on the seventh day. The connection between God's work and our rest is also made in Psalm 127. After explaining how foolish it is to work more and sleep less, Solomon says, "He who watches over you will not slumber; indeed, he who watches over Israel will neither slumber nor sleep" (Ps. 121:3–4). In times or places of danger, it is customary for people to set a watch. One person stays awake, looking for any sign of trouble, while the others try to get some sleep. The point the psalmist made is that God is always on the lookout. If we are with him, there is no sense staying up and worrying. We might as well go ahead and sleep, because God will be up all night watching anyway.

Solomon also said this: "[The Lord] grants sleep to those he loves" (Ps. 127:2). In other words, those who trust God will find their rest in his goodness and grace. This is a promise I often claim when I'm worn out. I say, "Lord, I'm so tired. But I know that you love me. Will you please show me your love by giving me the rest that I need." Of course, God's promise is not intended to compensate for my own sin. So when I stay up too late working, or when I fail to get enough sleep, I cannot expect God to deliver me from the physical and spiritual consequences of my disobedience. But as I trust him for everything, and as I live the way that he wants me to live, I can count on God to give me the rest I need. Jesus promised, "Come to me, all you who are weary and burdened, and I will give you rest" (Matt. 11:28).

# Part Three

# SCIENCE AND TECHNOLOGY

*What we may call the great theme—the belief that the cosmos is a sublimely harmonious system guided by a Supreme Intelligence, and that man has a place preordained and eternal in that system—runs through Western civilization. . . . [But] nowadays most scientists would accept the thesis that the cosmos has no underlying logic in the classical sense, but is rather a confluence of accidents, which are governed by laws. However, the laws themselves are irrational and do not arise from any fundamental orderliness.*

JAMIE JAMES

SCIENCE OWES A GREAT DEBT of gratitude to Christianity, because Christianity—more than any other worldview—established the principles that make science possible.

Christianity did this by making an absolute distinction between the Creator and his creation. Pagan cultures deified the creation, and thus regarded its scrutiny of as an act of impiety. By recognizing that the world is not divine, Christianity opened the door to scientific investigation. It also provided a rational basis for the orderliness of the cosmos: the universe was designed and made by an orderly God. This too was a necessary condition for science, because only an orderly universe is capable of being comprehended by rational minds like our own.

These basic principles of a Christian worldview legitimized the calling of the scientist. The astronomer Johannes Kepler acknowledged this when he wrote in one of his journals: "I give you thanks, Creator and God, that you have given me this joy in thy creation, and I rejoice in the works of your hands. See I have now completed the work to which I was called. In it I have used all the talents you have lent to my spirit."[1] In fulfillment of his calling to study creation, Kepler was fulfilling the chief end of science, which is to glorify God by enjoying what he has made.

Astronomers and other scientists are still exploring the uncharted frontiers of creation, but not always with Kepler's sense of sacred calling or spirit of holy worship. What is more common today is for scientists to claim almost divine authority over the creation and its inherent possibilities. We see this in the use of science for the destruction of human life. We see it in the genetic and technological modification of the human body—the quest for *technosapiens*. And we see it in the frequent disregard for the ethical boundaries of research. Like everyone else, scientists have a hard time resisting the allure of God-like control over their environment.

The essays in this section are based on a Christian approach to science and technology. This approach refuses to deify either the creation itself or the creatures who study it, but seeks instead to restore humility and reverence at the boundaries of life.

# 13

# RU CRAZY?

I first heard about RU-486 at a national pro-life rally in Washington, D.C. There I saw a man wearing a white T-shirt with large black letters that read "RU-486," followed by a question mark. The answer was on the back. It read, "RU Crazy?"

Apparently the Food and Drug Administration *is* crazy, because it has approved RU-486 for use in the United States. The drug is designed to induce an abortion. It is commonly called "the morning after pill" because it is primarily designed to deal with the consequences of sexual promiscuity. Actually, it is a series of pills taken over a period of several days, followed by another visit to the doctor two weeks later.

The new drug is almost certain to revolutionize abortion in America. For one thing, it will make abortion much more widely available. According to FDA regulations, virtually any family doctor will be able to prescribe RU-486. Recent surveys show that as many as one third of doctors who presently do not perform abortions are willing to prescribe the new drug. This means that women will be able to have an abortion almost anywhere in the United States, hidden from public stigma in the privacy of their own homes.

Another difference is that RU-486 can be taken very early in pregnancy, when Americans generally have fewer reservations about taking a life. This undoubtedly will have a dramatic effect on the politics of abortion. At present, a majority of Americans still oppose abortion. But those who oppose it simply because they are repulsed by current procedures for causing it are likely to change their view. In the words of Dr. Thomas Purdon, who is president-elect of the American College of Obstetrics and Gynecology, RU-486 makes "the emotional and ethical barriers . . . easier to cross."

Crossing ethical barriers is precisely the issue. Christians have opposed bringing RU-486 to the United States since the 1980s, when the drug first became available in France. This opposition has tended to focus on medical issues rather than on ethical ones. Opponents of RU-486 have spoken of the painful and unpleasant side-effects suffered by mothers who use it: nausea, cramping, bleeding, infection, depression, and in some rare cases, death. These practical considerations have undoubtedly had some influence in delaying the introduction of RU-486 to America. However, the pharmaceutical industry has been effective at minimizing the drug's side effects, and the FDA now has no reservation about making it available to the general public. They have ruled that RU-486 is "safe and effective" (unless, of course, you happen to be an unborn person).

This shows the inherent limitations of defending a moral position with pragmatic arguments. Pragmatic arguments have their place in the abortion debate. On occasion they may even persuade some women not to have an abortion. However, Christians will not win the fight for life without persuading the conscience of the nation, and the conscience can only be moved by fundamental considerations of right and wrong. Abortion has always been a spiritual issue. One thinks of Margaret Sanger's famous declaration that "no woman can call herself free who does not own and control her own body." Since it is a spiritual issue, the question to ask about RU-486, or about any other method of abortion, is whether it is part of God's best plan for the people he has made in his image.

The moral argument against abortion begins with the recognition that life begins at conception. And since life *does* begin at conception, taking RU-486 is nothing less than the deliberate taking of a human life. Abortion advocates say that in the early days of a pregnancy, a fetus is just a clump of cells. In one sense that is true; however, they are cells that have been clumped together by God himself to form a new human person. From the very moment of conception, a child enters life's two most important relationships: a relationship with God as Creator, and a relationship with another human being—the mother who is supposed to give the child nourishment and protection.

To provide biblical support for the conviction that personhood begins at conception, Christians often appeal to Psalm 139, where David writes, "My frame was not hidden from you when I was made in the secret place. When I was woven together in the depths of the earth, your eyes saw my unformed body" (Ps. 139:15). What this verse teaches is that the formation of a human life requires an act of God in a mother's womb. The verb that David uses to describe this divine act is significant. He says that the fetus is *raqam*, or "woven," almost like fine fabric. What is interesting about this word is that it is used almost exclusively in the Bible to describe the veils and curtains of the tabernacle in the wilderness. For example, the screen that stretched across the doorway of that holy tent was the work of a *roqem*, a weaver (Ex. 26:36).

What this seems to suggest is that a mother's womb is sacred space. Just as the tabernacle was God's holy dwelling place, so also the womb is consecrated by God's work in weaving together a human person. And in the same way that the tabernacle was off-limits to any unholy intrusion, it is forbidden to disturb the inner sanctum of a mother's womb.

Every abortion is a kind of sacrilege. When a mother and her doctor conspire to administer poison to an unborn child, they are violating a person that God has woven to be his dwelling-place. To see how dangerous this is, consider the following warning from Scripture: "If anyone destroys God's temple, God will destroy him; for God's temple is sacred, and you are that temple" (1 Cor. 3:17).[1]

# 14

# INTELLIGENT DESIGN

There has been a growing movement among scientists to recognize that the universe is the product of some intelligence. These scientists think they can show that various natural phenomena were deliberately designed. They are convinced that there is good scientific evidence for a guiding intelligence behind the origin and development of life.

Many of the scientists involved in the Intelligent Design movement, as it is called, are specialists in information theory. Information theory analyzes the way that information gets communicated from one place to another. By measuring the information expressed in natural processes and in living organisms, it is possible to determine whether that information came from an intelligent source. Intelligent causes can do things that undirected natural causes cannot. Or at least this is what the Intelligent Design movement argues.

Several branches of science have long made use of information theory. One is archaeology. When archaeologists dig at a site, they are looking for evidence that what they are finding is the result of intelligent human activity. To give an obvious example, archaeologists have scientific certainty that the ring of giant stones at Stonehenge is not a natural occurrence, but the product of intelligent design. Forensic scientists follow much the same line of reasoning. As they investigate a crime, they are looking for patterns that expose the work of a criminal mind.

Now the basic principles of information theory are also being used in biology, chemistry, and physics. Intelligent Design theorists point out that many natural systems are too intricate to be merely the product of chance. They contain information-rich structures that can only be the product of intelligent design. For example, biologists who study genetics see that DNA contains complex specified information—exactly the kind of information produced by a designing intelligence.

Intelligent Design is a direct challenge to the reigning scientific worldview, which is Darwinism, or evolutionism. Perhaps a better word for this worldview is naturalism. It is the belief—notice I use the word "belief"—that undirected, undesigned causes are totally responsible for the origin and development of life. The full diversity and complexity of life is produced by exclusively natural causes. So from the beginning, naturalists rule out the possibility of intelligent design because in their view, that would be unscientific. According to Harvard Genetics Professor Richard Lewontin, "We exist as material beings in a material world, all of whose phenomena are the consequences of material relations among material entities." In other words, matter is all that matters. There is no God at all, or at least there is no evidence for his involvement in the universe. As Lewontin goes on to say, "We cannot allow a Divine Foot in the door."[1]

Because it poses a direct threat to the totalizing worldview of naturalism, Intelligent Design is starting to attract more attention. It is also starting to come under attack. Members of the Ohio School Board recently considered a proposal to include Intelligent Design in the state curriculum. In response, evolutionists complained that Intelligent Design is just creationism in disguise. But that is hardly the case. Many Intelligent Design theorists are not even Christians, and some are not religious at all. They simply identify the evidence showing that intelligence is present without specifying the nature or identity of that intelligence. But the evolutionists are right to be worried. If there *is* scientific evidence for Intelligent Design, then they will have to let God back in the door—not just his foot, but the whole divine leg!

What is the value of talking about Intelligent Design? After all, as Christians we already know that the universe is designed. We know this because we know the Designer. The Scripture says:

> The heavens declare the glory of God;
>> the skies proclaim the work of his hands.
> Day after day they pour forth speech;
>> night after night they display knowledge. (Ps. 19:1–2)

By the intelligence of their design, the heavens bear eloquent testimony to the skill of their Designer. They have been doing this since long before anyone heard of Charles Darwin: "Since the creation of the world God's invisible qualities—his eternal power and divine nature—have been clearly seen, being understood from what has been made" (Rom. 1:20). But if we know that already, then why does it matter whether we can prove it by scientific means?

The answer is that Intelligent Design may be a useful tool for Christian apologetics. In addition to defending our own worldview, we have a responsibility to help other people recognize that their way of looking at the world is inadequate. Take the fabric of any non-Christian worldview, pull on its loose threads, and it will start to unravel.

That is what the Intelligent Design movement is trying to do with evolutionary naturalism. Many scientists fervently believe that the universe is the product of random chance rather than intelligent design. But if there is a way to demonstrate that the universe is really the product of design, then the first premise of naturalism is proven false. Intelligent Design theorists are trying to make that demonstration, and they are trying to do it on a scientific basis. In other words, they are trying to beat the naturalists at their own game, showing that naturalism fails on its own terms. If they can succeed in showing that there are scientific reasons to reject naturalism, then scientists and the people who listen to them will need to find a more adequate worldview, one that includes an explanation of who designed the universe the way that he did.[2]

# THE DOPAMINE
# MADE ME DO IT

"The dopamine made me do it." This is what the addicts and the crim-
inals will say once they read a study out of the Brookhaven National
Laboratory in New York, where a research team published evidence that
what makes people get high on cocaine is a surge of dopamine.[1]

Dopamine is a neurotransmitter. In other words, it is a molecule that
delivers messages from one neuron in the brain to another. The message
dopamine usually delivers is the one that tells the brain "Yay!" Dopamine
makes us feel euphoric.

According to the new theory of addiction, addicts are not addicted
to drugs, or gambling, or pornography so much as they are addicted to
dopamine. And almost any pleasurable experience can give us a surge of
the stuff: getting a hug, receiving a promotion, eating a piece of choco-
late cake, making a three-point basket, anything. What is different about
drugs is that they dump so much dopamine on someone's system it is
hard to absorb it all, so it just keeps running around the brain.

Dopamine is only the latest attempt to say that human beings are
little more than bodies. Scientists and others often try to reduce persons

to strands of DNA or bags of chemicals. We do not make moral choices any more; we are simply controlled by our physical impulses.

An article by Tom Wolfe, author of *The Bonfire of the Vanities,* concludes that what we are witnessing is nothing less than the death of the soul.[2] According to Wolfe, the twentieth century witnessed the death of God. He does not mean that God has actually died, but that God no longer matters to Western culture. The twenty-first century, Wolfe says, will witness the death of the soul.

In the past, Westerners believed that they had souls as well as bodies. The Children's Catechism asks, "Do you have a soul as well as a body?" "Yes," the answer goes, "I have a soul that can never die." But many scientists now argue that human beings do not have souls, only bodies. Our thoughts, ideas, feelings, and emotions are not states of mind, they are just states of brain. Our biology is our destiny.

One of the consequences of the death of the soul is that people can no longer be held responsible for their actions. Alcoholics, drug addicts, gamblers, and others now protest that their problems are simply "diseases" which need "treatment."

Lawyers mounted a similar defense on behalf of Craig Rabinowitz, who was charged with murdering his wife to pay off debts incurred by an exotic dancer. His lawyers said what Rabinowitz did was "against human nature." In other words, something must be wrong with the man's chemistry. The dopamine made him do it.

What does the Bible teach about the sins of the flesh? For starters, the Bible recognizes that our bodies have a lot to do with the way we sin. The apostle Paul did not know about dopamine, but he understood the way sin reigns in our mortal bodies (Rom. 6:12). He knew that our physical appetites bring us under bondage to sin. The more we use our bodies to sin, the more enslaved to sin we become. Paul did not talk about "addiction" in so many words, but he did speak of the "body of sin" (Rom. 6:6).

Even though our bodies are wrapped up in our sins, God continues to hold us responsible for what we do with our bodies. Jesus taught that both the soul and the body contribute to sin: "You have heard that it was said, 'Do not commit adultery.' But I tell you that anyone who looks at a woman lustfully has already committed adultery with her in his heart" (Matt. 5:27–28). Jesus went right to the heart of the matter: sin is rooted in the soul.

Once the soul decides to sin, the body starts to take over. Very likely, even if it is not the whole story, dopamine has something to do with the way the sins of the heart become the sins of the flesh. But however pleasurable it is, Jesus says we are still guilty for our sin. "If your right hand causes you to sin," he says, "cut it off and throw it away. It is better for you to lose one part of your body than for your whole body to go into hell" (Matt. 5:30). It is often suggested that Jesus was exaggerating here to make a point. No doubt Jesus *was* trying to make a point. But part of his point is that the soul is not the body's victim. Sometimes we become so enslaved to the temptations of the flesh that we feel powerless to resist them. But if the Spirit of God lives in us we are not powerless. We have the same incomparably great power at work in us that raised Christ from the dead (Eph. 1:19–20). Now that spiritual power is at work to transform both our souls and our bodies.

If we were dominated by dopamine, no one could ever be delivered from sins of addiction. But the Spirit of God brings deliverance from drug abuse, alcoholism, gambling, sexual addiction, and a host of other sins of the flesh. Usually, this does not happen overnight. But it will and it must happen eventually for every child of God: "For we know that our old self was crucified with [Christ] so that the body of sin might be done away with. . . . Do not offer the parts of your body to sin, as instruments of wickedness, but rather offer yourselves to God . . . and offer the parts of your body to him as instruments of righteousness" (Rom. 6:6, 12).

# 16

# THE GOD
# OF THE GENOME

In June 2000 scientists announced the first big discovery of the new millennium. For years two teams of scientists had been racing to decipher the bits of DNA that comprise the human genetic code. Finally, Francis Collins, who directs the National Genome Research Institute, and Craig Venter, the maverick CEO of a private firm for scientific research, joined forces to announce that the genome race was over.

What these scientists had discovered was the biochemical code for human genes, the complete set of instructions for constructing and maintaining a fully operational human being. First they had taken DNA from human chromosomes and shredded it into short segments. Then they began to use a supercomputer to reassemble the DNA by matching all the overlapping segments. The result is an unpunctuated genetic sentence more than three billion letters long.

The genome assembly is almost complete, but there is still a great deal of work to be done. Scientists are now working to identify all the genes within the genome, and also to map them in their proper sequence. It will take them even longer to determine what the genes do. To give a simple analogy, they now have a book with all the letters in the right order, but the words still have to be decoded. Figuring out what they mean will be something like reading a book in an unknown foreign language.

Mapping the human genome will lead to rapid changes in the field of medicine. Indeed, within the next several decades the practice of medicine may be completely transformed. There will be new ways to diagnose and treat diseases. Personalized gene therapy may even help to prevent certain diseases, especially genetic ones.

It will be years before we understand the implications of this scientific breakthrough, but some important ethical questions are already being raised. Is it appropriate for companies to patent sections of human DNA? Will insurance companies use genetic information to deny coverage to people who are susceptible to particular diseases? Will parents alter the genetic code to produce designer children?

As important as these questions are, the question that interests me the most is theological: What, if anything, does the deciphering of the human genome reveal about the mind and character of God? The day that the discovery was announced, President Clinton said, "Today we are learning the language in which God created life." Of course, if he had been teaching science in a public high school, Mr. Clinton never would have been able to say that, but he was right nonetheless. The genome is the language in which God created life. And if that is true, then it must have something to tell us about the God who invented it.

The Bible teaches that "since the creation of the world God's invisible qualities—his eternal power and divine nature—have been clearly seen, being understood from what has been made, so that men are without excuse" (Rom. 1:20). This verse provides the foundation for a doctrine of general revelation, which simply means that in a general way God has revealed himself in everything that he has made. This is true not only of large things, like the earth and the sun, but also of small things, like the microscopic strands of DNA that comprise the human genome.

The human genome shows that God is orderly. Back in the eighteenth century William Paley (1743–1805) tried to prove the existence of God from the way that the universe is designed. This is sometimes called "the argument from design." Paley made a good case, but he didn't know the half of it. The discoveries of the twentieth century—and now the twenty-first century—have only served to confirm God's amazing ability to design living things of astonishing intricacy. It will take molecular biologists a long, long time to unlock all the mysteries of the human genome, but what we already know is enough to demonstrate God's ability to design a network of living systems that actually works.

With its billions and billions of letters, the genome is extraordinarily complex. Could it be the product of mere probability? Not a chance! God has left his fingerprint on our DNA, every strand of which is a testimony to his wisdom and knowledge. As Dr. Collins said when he made his historic announcement, "It is humbling for me and awe-inspiring to realize that we have caught the first glimpse of our own instruction book, previously known only to God."

The human genome also shows that God is omniscient. For all the discoveries that they have made, scientists have yet to exhaust the mind of God. The more we know about the world that God has made, the more amazed we are. Rather than discovering design flaws somewhere in the universe, we are continually reminded that God's capacity to create exceeds our capacity to discover. As scientists decode the human genome, we are reminded once again that we are "fearfully and wonderfully made" (Ps. 139:14) by an awesome and wonderful Creator.

The human genome can teach us many things about the mind of the Maker. But human beings are much more than simply a set of genetic instructions. It takes more than molecular biology to explain the mysterious bond that develops between a mother and her newborn child, or the sense of awe that a worshiper feels when drawn into the presence of God. It takes a theologian to explain these things—a theologian who knows that human beings are more than just strands of genetic code. We are "fearfully and wonderfully made" because we are made in the image and likeness of God. This gives us the capacity to know and be known, to love and be loved, so that we might declare our Maker's praise.[1]

# 17

# HERE A SHEEP, THERE A SHEEP, EVERYWHERE A SHEEP, SHEEP

Scientists at Scotland's Roslin Institute recently unveiled a seven-month-old sheep that was an exact genetic replica of her mother. Here is how they did it. First, they removed cells from the udder of an adult sheep, a white Finn Dorset ewe. Each cell was immersed in chemicals to make it dormant and stop it from dividing. Meanwhile, an unfertilized egg cell was taken from a Scottish Blackface ewe. The nucleus of the egg cell was extracted, including its DNA. Then the two cells were placed next to one another and charged with an electric pulse to fuse them together. A second electrical pulse reactivated the DNA from the original sheep and the cell began to grow and divide.

A week later the new embryo was implanted in the uterus of yet a third Blackface sheep. After gestation, the surrogate mother gave birth to a lamb named Dolly. There are no genetic similarities between the lamb and its Blackface birth mother. Instead, the lamb is genetically identical to the Finn Dorset from which the DNA was originally taken.

This is not the first time scientists have been able to make a clone. Beginning in the 1950s they have cloned frogs, pigs, cows, and monkeys. But up until now the clones have only been made from embryos. What is unique about Dolly is that she was cloned from the genetic material of an *adult* mammal.

The cloning of a mature animal raises dozens of scientific, ethical, and spiritual questions. The first question one asks is "Will there ever be another me?" In other words, "Is it possible to clone a human being?" Scientists speculate that it is now theoretically possible to use the same technique on human beings. But we will not know for certain until someone actually does it.

Scientists involved in cloning research are quick to dismiss the possibility of human clones. They have no intention of cloning human beings, they say. There is no good reason for anyone to try it, they say. Ian Wilmut, the mastermind behind the sheep clone, is not worried about the possibility because he believes that "we are a moral species." But such scientists are extremely naïve about human depravity. What we are is an *immoral* species. Of course someone will try to clone a human being, if only to be the first one to do it. Someone, somewhere, will be unable to resist the notoriety of cloning another human being . . . or himself.

Would a human clone still be made in the image of God? Yes, of course. A clone would be able to sing the words of Psalm 139 with full confidence:

> For you created my inmost being;
>     you knit me together in my mother's womb.
> I praise you because I am fearfully and wonderfully made;
>     your works are wonderful,
>     I know that full well.
> My frame was not hidden from you
>     when I was made in the secret place.
> When I was woven together in the depths of the earth,
>     your eyes saw my unformed body. (Ps. 139:13–16)

Scientific procedures are not exempt from the creative providence of God. Clone or no clone, a human being with a mind, a heart, and especially a soul is a person made in the image of God.

Furthermore, a human clone would still be a unique individual. A person is vastly more than the sum total of his or her DNA. Clones would be different persons because they would have different experiences. Since they would be born at different times, they would be even less identical than identical twins, and anyone who knows identical twins knows that they are their own persons. Twins also make their own spiritual choices, as Jacob and Esau so powerfully demonstrate (Gen. 25:21–28; cf. Rom. 9:10–12). It may turn out to be possible to clone human DNA, but it will never be possible to clone a human *person*.

Would it be wrong to clone a human being? Americans are instinctively opposed to the idea, and President Clinton followed the lead of several European nations by banning the use of federal funds for research on human cloning. We feel as if cloning is wrong, but why is it wrong?

One biblical principle that explains why cloning a human being would be wrong is the principle of "one flesh." The Bible says about marriage: "A man will leave his father and mother and be united to his wife, and they will become one flesh" (Gen. 2:24). The cloning of a human being violates this one-flesh principle. Either a clone has no biological father or it has no biological mother. As a cell biologist from Missouri observed, if cloning were perfected, "there'd be no need for men." Instead of producing a new human being out of the union of a man and a woman, cloning would simply reproduce the man or the woman.

God's design for procreation is infinitely more fascinating than cloning, not to mention more pleasurable. Instead of simply replicating one person's genes, God produces an entirely new person out of the combination of two people. And he uses sexual intercourse to do it. Scientists are the ones bringing us reproduction without sex, not God.

Another reason why trying to clone a human being would be immoral is that it would involve the wanton destruction of human embryos. Dolly was the lucky one. She beat the odds. Nearly 300 cells were taken from her mother and implanted in egg cells from other sheep. Out of 277 tries only twenty-nine embryos survived a week or more. And of those twenty-nine embryos, only one made it to birth. The rest were defective, abnormal, or sick. They were wasted along the way. Furthermore, scientists have since discovered that Dolly and other animal clones have increased health problems and decreased life spans. To cause such harm to sheep is to take bad care of creation. To do them to human beings would be monstrous.

# 18

# I'LL SEND MY SOS
# TO THE WORLD

New modes of communication always have implications for how we share the gospel. In the church, email has revolutionized the prayer request.

Personal prayer requests used to be shared by word of mouth, mainly within the confines of a local congregation. No longer. There have always been letters, of course—especially missionary prayer letters. Then came the telephone, and with it the prayer chain. But now, with the click of a button, it is possible to send prayer requests all over the world. A number of on-line locations now serve as clearing houses for anyone seeking intercession.

Generally, this is a wonderful development, although I don't know that it necessarily improves the efficacy of our prayers. God has an amazing ability to answer general requests in specific ways. His Spirit often prompts people to pray about exactly what needs to be prayed for, even when the one praying and the one who needs prayer are separated by time and distance. So God has not been waiting around for the information revolution. But electronic mail still strengthens our bonds of fellowship. In some situations, it enables more people to pray more intelligently. By spreading prayer news around the world, the Internet helps us meet the biblical goal of praying continually (1 Thess. 5:17). And it is encouraging to know that people will be praying for us right when we need their prayers.

For all its advantages, e-prayer has also caused some problems, mainly through the global invasion of personal privacy. In March of 2001 *The Wall Street Journal* ran a story entitled, "If No One Has Linked You to a Prayer Chain, Count Your Blessings—People with Problems Can Find Their Names and Woes Aired on Well-Meaning Web Sites."

The article documented the difficulties of a missionary from Dallas. The poor man had picked up a parasite in Thailand, and for several years he struggled with poor health, losing more than a hundred pounds in the process. At a certain point he sent out an intensely private message, explaining not only his unpleasant symptoms, but also his feelings of spiritual despair. With the best of intentions, some of his supporters forwarded his request to several prayer sites on the Internet. Someone added a statement to the effect that unless God intervened, the missionary had only two months to live.

The man was happy enough to be prayed for, of course—and also to receive some financial support, as the checks started rolling in—but he was embarrassed and a little offended by all the attention. To date he has received more than 10,000 emails and 2,000 personal letters. And since old prayer requests never die, copies of his original prayer request are still bouncing around cyberspace. People still call the missionary's church and say, "I hear that old so-and-so's on his deathbed again."

There have been other, less dramatic cases. People have requested prayer for alcoholic spouses, friends with breast cancer, and pregnant teenagers—not anonymously, but giving their full names. There have also been hoaxes. Every few months another Christian legend seems to surface: a missionary held hostage, a Third World evangelist falsely accused of a capital crime, a pastor on life support. One fall I kept receiving the same urgent message to pray for missionaries in Africa—a request we knew to be false because it had been disavowed by the mission agency that was mentioned.

With some of these problems in mind, I offer the following guidelines for Christian "Netiquette":

First, get permission. Before you forward someone else's prayer request, be sure to get their consent.

Second, get the facts straight. Particularly if you are forwarding a prayer request on someone else's behalf, be sure to verify that you have the latest, most accurate information. Resist the urge to embellish the story, make inferences, or draw your own conclusions.

Third, be discreet. Remember that once you send out a request, you have little or no control over where it goes. If you are sharing a need with a distribution list, include only those details that can be shared with the general public. Be careful to preserve confidentiality.

Fourth, if you receive prayer requests over a general list, be sure to get permission before using the list for your own prayer requests. This is part of Christian kindness. Many Internet users are inundated with email, and they may or may not want to know about your need. Keep in mind that people on the same list do not always know one another. Sharing your needs with people you don't know is a little bit like dropping in unannounced.

Fifth, be sure to send an update. People do a better job of circulating requests than they do of sharing outcomes. Once a crisis passes it is easy to forget that other people are still praying. They will be encouraged to know how God has worked in a situation, so be sure to let them know.

Finally, when you get a prayer request, be sure actually to pray. For Christians, email is not simply a good way of finding out what is happening in the church. It is meant to be a stimulus to intercession. When you get a prayer update, either pray for it right away or print out a hard copy to keep with the rest of your prayer notes. Figure out what works best for you, but whatever you do, don't just read the request; pray for it!

# Part Four

# SOCIAL ISSUES

*According to the arrangement of God, the Christian is more of
a Christian in society than alone, and more in the enjoyment
of privileges of a spiritual kind when he shares them with others,
than when he possesses them apart. . . . The Christian Church was
established in the world, to realize the superior advantages of
a social over an individual Christianity, and to set up
and maintain the communion of the saints.*

JAMES BANNERMAN

AMERICAN EVANGELICALS PLACE a high priority on having a personal relationship with Jesus Christ. There is something right about this. Salvation only comes through Christ, who can only be received by faith. This faith must be personal to be genuine. We become Christians by owning up to our rebellion against God and trusting that when Jesus died on the cross, it was for our own sins as much as for anyone else's.

What we sometimes fail to recognize is that there is also a corporate dimension to our salvation. The redemption that we have in Christ is a gift that we share with all other Christians. We are all united to Christ, so whatever God has done to save any one of us he has done to save all of us. The theological term for this is "the communion of the saints." We belong to what Martin Luther described as "a community of pure saints . . . called together by the Holy Spirit in one faith, mind, and understanding."[1]

The community that we have in Christ naturally gives us an interest in human society. We are concerned about the structures of human relationships, not simply because they affect us as individuals, but because we know the transforming power of the gospel. We know this because we have experienced it in our relationships in the church, where there is "neither Jew nor Greek, slave nor free, male nor female, for you are all one in Christ Jesus" (Gal. 3:28).

Despite its commitment to community, the church has often been slow to speak out against racism, sexism, individualism, and other social problems. This has done serious damage to our witness. Secular culture has filled the void by addressing these issues, but without the biblical values that are necessary for making real social progress. As a result, some Christians have concluded that the pursuit of social justice is itself a secular ideal, when in fact it is thoroughly biblical.

God has called us to live out our faith in committed, reconciled relationships that have a transforming influence on social structures. The proper Christian approach is not to shy away from social problems, but to address them in a positive way that shows the hope of community in Christ.

# 19

# THE COLOR LINE

When it comes to race relations in the United States, I am generally an optimist. I can afford that luxury, of course, because I belong to America's ethnic majority—at least for the time being. But no matter how far we still have to go, it must be said that we have come a long way. We have come a long way from the Tulsa race riots of the 1920s, from Negro League baseball in the 1940s, from *Brown v. Board of Education* in the 1950s, and even from the civil-rights movement of the 1960s. Minorities have more opportunities and Americans generally have greater exposure to other cultures than ever before.

I may be an optimist, but I am also a Calvinist, and that means that I believe in total depravity. I am not surprised, therefore, when race relations take a step backward, as they often do. Every time it seems as if we are making some progress, something happens to remind us of how far we still have to go. We hear an ugly racial slur, we sense a racist undercurrent at a child's sporting event, or we read about an act of racially motivated violence. And then we remember that we belong to a fallen and divided race.

One leading indicator of racial attitudes in America has always been housing. Where people live, and with whom, tells us something about how well they get along. Figures from the 2000 United States Census point to a somewhat unexpected result.

As everyone knows, our country is becoming more and more ethnically diverse. Yet as far as housing is concerned, it remains as segregated as ever, if not more so. Despite the fact that many minorities are moving to the suburbs, the color lines are still being drawn. Professor John Logan, who directs the Lewis Mumford Center for Comparative Urban and Regional Research, concludes that although we "might have thought the black civil-rights movement or the rise of the black middle class or changing racial attitudes surely by now would have made a difference," the truth is that "the color line is still very strong." Whether we are black or white, yellow or brown, we are choosing to live with people of our own kind.

Racism is one area where actions have a way of speaking louder than words. Many people say that they are more accepting of people from other ethnic backgrounds. They also say that they are seeking to have more diverse friendships. Yet when it comes to deciding where to live, they tend to stay in their own communities. According to one journalist, the census suggests "that four decades of efforts to integrate communities have largely failed. While other research suggests that racial attitudes with regard to housing have lessened, actual settlement patterns remain rooted in the past. Children of the early 21st century will likely grow up isolated from people of other ethnic groups—much as the children of the early 20th century did."

This kind of segregation used to be the result of overtly racist housing policies. As W. E. B. DuBois thoroughly documented in his landmark study, *The Philadelphia Negro,* the practice of real estate redlining helped turn many Philadelphia neighborhoods into ghettos. During the early decades of the twentieth century, banks and other lending institutions drew boundaries around certain urban areas, refusing to issue loans for property within those boundaries. All of the neighborhoods were black. Those policies have long since been lifted. However, even when people have more freedom to choose where they want to live, they are still following the lines.

This should remind us that racial reconciliation does not happen on its own. It requires us to make intentional choices about what we do, where we go, with whom we associate—even where we live. Unless we decide to cross some of the usual boundaries, we will always stay within the lines.

One place where we ought to be crossing boundaries is the church. The Bible says, "There is neither Jew nor Greek, slave nor free, male nor female, for you are all one in Christ Jesus" (Gal. 3:28). This verse does not obliterate real social distinctions based on ethnicity, class, and gender. Yet it insists that we have a fundamental unity in Christ that keeps those distinctions from dividing us. God's Spirit is at work to bring us together in Christ.

This raises a very practical question: What kind of relationships are you forming? How does your life demonstrate the truth that God is making one new people in Christ? This is not simply a black and white issue, because skin color is not the only thing that divides us. We are divided by culture, education, economics, and even social class. These barriers can only be crossed by the love of Christ working in us to help us know and care for those who are different from us.

We are also divided by nationality. How many internationals do you know? How many do you know *well?* How many of your friendships cross ethnic and cultural boundaries? What about your dinner invitations? Are we spending time together in contexts that can lead to genuine friendship and fellowship?

As Christians, we have a remarkable opportunity to know people from many different ethnic and cultural backgrounds. We can worship together, which is a foretaste of heaven, when people from "every nation, tribe, people and language" will gather at God's throne (Rev. 7:9). But we can do more than worship together. We can also know one another. We can care for one another. And we can love one another, showing the world that there is no color line in the kingdom of God.[1]

## 20

# FACE TO FACE

In 2001 *Time* magazine published a fascinating photo essay featuring the faces of Afghan women. The women had only recently been liberated from the Taliban by the combined efforts of the Northern Alliance and the United States Air Force. Finally they were free to take off their *burqas,* the long, dark veils that had masked their identity under the guise of true religion. The photographs lifted the veil to uncover faces that were fresh and jubilant, defiantly beautiful.

I have seen *burqas* before. Occasionally one sees them in Philadelphia—on the street, by the bus stop, and at the shopping market. According to the strictest interpretation of Islamic law, or *Shari'a,* a woman's *burqa* is required to cover not only her face, but her whole body from head to toe. The only part of the garment that is open is the thick mesh that permits a woman to breathe and to a certain extent to see, but not to be seen.

I have generally looked at *burqas* as something of a curiosity. They seemed strange, but essentially harmless—a different way to dress. It had not occurred to me until seeing the photos from Afghanistan how dangerous they are, that in fact they are deeply destructive of human personhood.

The *burqa* is a sign of the extreme evil of Islamic extremism. For five years, women in Kabul and elsewhere had been forbidden to show their faces in public. Imagine going for half a decade without anyone seeing you, and therefore without knowing you in one of the most intimate ways that you can be known: by face. To be prevented from knowing and being known in this way is an assault on human dignity and community.

Perhaps some Muslims would respond by saying that many women choose to wear *burqas*. I doubt whether this is true. According to one secret survey, as many as ninety-five percent of Afghan women would prefer not to wear a *burqa*. But even if some women choose to wear them, it makes the situation all the sadder because it means that oppression had penetrated the whole structure of Afghan society.

By attempting to blot out women's faces, the Taliban attempted to deny their individuality. For five years many women had been under virtual house arrest. Some did not own *burqas*, and thus were prevented from leaving their homes. Even worse, the *burqa* created a climate in which other, more severe forms of oppression became common. Afghan women were denied education. They had virtually no access to health care. And if they violated Islamic law, they were subject to physical punishment in the form of public beatings.

All of this degradation comes from a real hatred against women. Naturally, it had a profoundly negative effect on the physical, emotional, and spiritual welfare of Afghan women. There were credible reports of Taliban soldiers routinely engaging in rape and other acts of violence against women. None of this is surprising; it is simply the *burqa* taken to its logical extreme.

No wonder some women tore off their veils and danced in the streets when the Taliban left Kabul. One can only imagine the joy that they now experience in seeing and being seen face to face. One woman said, "When I heard the Taliban was finished I rejoiced beyond measure. . . . Now I see the sunlight and it's so beautiful."

The *burqa* is not only an offense against humanity, but also a crime against God, who made women in his image (Gen. 1:27). God's true intention is for us to honor his image by seeing and knowing one another face to face. This is true in all our relationships. It is true professionally.

Anyone who wants to get anywhere in business or politics needs "face time"—personal interaction with people of power and influence.

Face time is especially important in the family. The joy of marriage is having someone to live with face to face, a lover and a friend. This is the same way that parents know their children: face to face. I once read that on average American children spend less than three minutes a day face-to-face with their fathers. Ever since learning that sad fact I have made it a special point not simply to spend time with my children, but also whenever possible to look them in the eye. This is how a father knows his children: by studying the subtle changes in their countenance. And this is how children know their father: by gazing upon his face, where they see the sternness of his rebuke and the tenderness of his love.

To know someone face-to-face is to know that person with true intimacy. This is why it is so amazing that God offers us such knowledge of himself. "Now we see but a poor reflection as in a mirror," the Scripture says. "Then we shall see face to face" (1 Cor. 13:12).

This is among the most precious of all God's promises. There is something metaphoric about it, of course, but we should not dismiss its literal dimension. The Bible promises that one day we will see God's face (see Matt. 5:8; Rev. 22:4). We believe that Jesus rose again, bodily, and that therefore he retains his human nature in physical form. Therefore, when we get to heaven we will be able to gaze upon his very face. God has promised to give us the light of the knowledge of his glory in the face of Jesus Christ (2 Cor. 4:6). Theologians call this the "beatific vision." If only we knew our heart's true desire, we would know that his face is the one we have been looking for all these years. And we would know that seeing Jesus, face to face, will satisfy all our deepest longings.[1]

# THE LION, THE WITCH, AND THE BOARDROOM

More than fifty years ago C. S. Lewis published *The Lion, the Witch and the Wardrobe,* the first of seven children's books called the *Chronicles of Narnia.* The books have been a spectacular publishing success. They have also served as a wonderful tool for pre-evangelism. *The Lion, the Witch and the Wardrobe* is a story of betrayal, redemption, atonement, and resurrection. It is not quite a Christian allegory, but it does tell the story of the gospel. In fact, my grandmother used to read it to her public school students as a form of covert evangelism. I think Lewis himself would have approved. He once observed that his fantasies enabled Christian theology to "steal past those watchful dragons"—the enemies of orthodoxy.

Many Christians are passionate about Narnia, which explains the storm of protest when *The New York Times, The Boston Globe,* and other major newspapers reported on plans to update Lewis's literary legacy. There have been three major allegations: first, that the C. S. Lewis Company forced a PBS documentary to downplay Lewis's Christianity; second, that HarperCollins is planning to add new titles to the Narnia series;

and third, that the publisher is actively seeking to remove Christian imagery from Lewis's fiction.[1]

These accusations are based primarily on an internal memo written by Steve Hanselman, the editorial director at HarperCollins. The purpose of his memo was to make sure that the PBS special did not say too much about Lewis's personal faith in Jesus Christ. Hanselman wrote: "We'll need to be able to give emphatic assurances that no attempt will be made to correlate the [Narnia] stories to Christian imagery/theology . . . the documentary should not make this connection in any way. Narnia should come across as one of the great creations of fantasy literature, with roots in general myth and folklore."

Hanselman also commented on the film's approach to Lewis's conversion. "This drives the narrative," he wrote, "how he [Lewis] grows to maturity and passes from atheism, to skepticism, to belief—but is not overdone so as to cause worry. As treated, there is no characterization of what 'true conversion' or 'true Christianity' is supposed to be. We'll need to make sure it stays that way."

These comments do not come as much of a surprise to C. S. Lewis experts. The people who now control Lewis's publications often seem more interested in making money and protecting their literary property than in furthering the cause of the gospel that Lewis loved. So what kinds of changes can we expect?

Apparently trying to capitalize on the success of Harry Potter, HarperCollins proposed publishing new Narnia books, written by new authors. According to the president of the children's division, these books "will not be sequels as such, but books using the same characters and with story lines which fill in the gaps of existing ones." (It must be said that any writer who attempts to reproduce the work of a literary giant like C. S. Lewis is a fool.)

It seems doubtful whether anyone will attempt to change the books that Lewis has already written. HarperCollins bristles at the suggestion that it has any intention of tampering with Lewis's legacy. The publisher has spent millions of dollars to reissue and promote Lewis's nonfiction, and is eager to show that its new editions are faithful to the originals. Indeed,

HarperCollins has done the church a service by printing books such as *Mere Christianity* in a way that will attract a new and wider audience.

What is striking about all of this is the blatant hostility that some people are showing to the gospel. Clearly, what they are opposed to is Jesus Christ. They seem to think that C. S. Lewis would be all right, if only something could be done about his Christianity. What makes this so laughable, of course, is that his faith is thoroughly integrated into all his work.

C. S. Lewis mastered several different kinds of writing: apologetics (*Mere Christianity*), autobiography (*Surprised by Joy, A Grief Observed* ), theology (*The Four Loves, Miracles, The Problem of Pain*), fantasy (the *Chronicles of Narnia*), and science fiction (*Perelandra, Out of the Silent Planet, That Hideous Strength*), to say nothing of his literary criticism. Lewis's scholarly books on medieval and Renaissance literature (such as *A Preface to Paradise Lost, Oxford History of English Literature—The Sixteenth Century, An Experiment in Criticism*) remain standard works in the field. Then there is his inventive work on demonology (*The Screwtape Letters*).

What ties all these works together is Lewis's faith in Jesus Christ. His Christian commitment informs his analysis, shapes his imagination, and guides his theology. Almost every page of his work speaks of the horrors of sin, the joy of salvation, and the duties of the Christian life. In response to the attempt to keep Jesus out of Narnia, *The New York Times Book Review* observed that "if Christianity is an obstacle, then the publisher has a problem . . . they are Christian through and through. It's not as if Lewis composed some children's stories, then sprinkled on a dusting of religious imagery that a sequel writer can easily sponge off. At every level except the most superficial, they're an explicit allegory of faith."[2] Remove the Christianity from the writings of C. S. Lewis and there would be nothing left!

In a culture that is increasingly resistant to good Christian thinking, C. S. Lewis continues to serve as a good model for our evangelism. In one of his letters he wrote of his aspiration to "say things helpful to salvation."[3] By doing this, he kept the biblical command: "Always be prepared to give an answer to everyone who asks you to give the reason for the hope that you have" (1 Peter 3:15). In his evangelism C. S. Lewis always made Jesus Christ the central issue. May God help us to live in such a way that people are always confronted with Christ, whether they will accept him or not.

# 22

# DOCTOR PHIL

Maybe it was the name: Doctor Phil. Or perhaps it was the way his face
kept showing up on the sides of buses and on national television. Suddenly Doctor Phil was everywhere—chatting with Oprah, analyzing Larry
King, and making a cameo on "Good Morning, America." It could have
been his no-nonsense style, the aggressive way that he told total strangers
to get their act together. Or maybe it was the title of his latest book, the
#1 bestseller *Self Matters*. But for whatever reason, I decided it was time
to read America's most famous psychologist, Dr. Phillip C. McGraw.

*Self Matters* begins with a sort of conversion story. McGraw tells how
unhappy he was during his early years in counseling: "I knew I wasn't
living the life I was meant to live. I knew there was something wrong
with my life, but for those ten years, I avoided dealing with it." What
was the problem? Basically, Doctor Phil wasn't being true to himself.
Instead, he was always trying to meet other people's expectations. "I
ignored my self," he writes, "and lived for people, purposes, and goals
that weren't my own. I betrayed who I was and instead accepted a fic-
tional substitute that was defined from the outside in."[1]

The way Doctor Phil solved his problems was by working from the
inside out, which is what he tells his readers to do, too. The way to
become the person you were always meant to be is to listen to your inward

voice, to connect with your "authentic self"—the real you. It's about self-acceptance. It's about self-awareness: "You have to get intimately in touch with you." It's also about self-affirmation, or believing "your personal truth," which is what "you have come to believe about you." "The 'fix' I'm talking about," writes Doctor Phil, "always deals with you being true to yourself from the inside out."

The reason this approach to life works—according to Dr. McGraw—is because you have within yourself all the resources you need for every situation in life. He writes: "Every one of us, you included, has within us everything we will ever need to be, do, and have anything and everything we will ever want and need." This is a staggering claim, one that deifies the self, placing you at the center of your universe.

It's not hard to understand why Dr. McGraw is so popular. For starters, Americans have always believed in the self. Our real motto is not "In God We Trust," but "Trust Thyself."[2] We also like to be in charge, and Doctor Phil promises that if we follow his advice, we will "control virtually every aspect of [our] experience in this world."

*Self Matters* says nothing about Christianity, and almost nothing about religion in general. On those rare occasions when Doctor Phil does mention God, it is usually to take his name in vain. However, he is still taking a theological position. By saying that the self is what matters, he is pulling God off his throne.

The most surprising thing about Dr. McGraw's book is how familiar it all sounds. There's a new face and a new attitude, but it's the same old conventional psychology, with the same old talk about self-help and self-image. What is so tragic is that Doctor Phil is moving people in exactly the wrong direction. The more self-absorbed we become, the less able we are to worship God or to serve others. To put this another way, the more we love our selves, the more difficult it is for us to keep the two great commandments: love God and love your neighbor (Matt. 22:37–39). It is true that Jesus said, "Love your neighbor *as yourself*" (Matt. 22:39). However, by saying this he was not encouraging us to become self-absorbed. Rather, he was telling us to love others with the same instinctive concern that we have for our own needs.

The Bible says, "Do not think of yourself more highly than you ought" (Rom. 12:3). It also says, "Consider others better than yourselves," not looking after your own interests, but after theirs (Phil. 2:3–4). This is the pattern Jesus set for us when he came to suffer and to die for our sins. It is only when we follow his example—living for others rather than for ourselves—that we discover our true purpose in life. So rather than helping people find their true identity, Doctor Phil actually is keeping them from it.

There are also serious problems with his idea that we need to stop accepting the roles that other people have for us. It's true that it can be unhealthy to try to live up to other people's expectations. However, it is right and good for us to be defined by our positions in life. I am a husband, a father, a pastor, and a friend. These are God-given callings that require me to live for others instead of myself. Rather than preventing me from finding my true self, they help me become the self that God wants me to become.

The last thing to say about *Self Matters* is that it's not our responsibility to create our lives from the inside out. And it's a good thing, too! Our lives, with all our talents and abilities, with all our obstacles and opportunities, are given to us by God. So if anyone is going to help us from the inside out, it is going to be God's Spirit. The way we find our true identity is not by turning inward, but by being baptized into Jesus Christ. Once we are in Christ, the Holy Spirit works in our lives, enabling us to look outside ourselves to others. It is by serving them that we will fulfill our true purpose, becoming the children of God that we are called to become.

# 23

# HEROIN CHIC

They may look like drug addicts, but in 1996 they became a major trend in the fashion industry: models who are emaciated, dirty, and untidy. The look is called heroin chic. The models strut down the catwalk, or stare defiantly from billboards and magazine spreads. They wear clothes by the top names in fashion design, names like Calvin Klein, Gianni Versace, and Karl Lagerfeld.

The reason the models look like drug addicts is that they are *supposed* to look like drug addicts. The models were selected because they are scrawny and pale: "They flaunt the ominous signs of drug addiction: vacant stares, dirty disheveled hair, unkempt clothes and a frame so gaunt, bone juts through flesh."[1] Then they are coached to look and behave like heroin addicts, hence the name "heroin chic." Their eyelids are half-closed and they stagger slightly as they walk.

Many of the models who sport the heroin look have tattoos. Others wear pierced jewelry in unusual places—through the nose, on the chest, or in the bellybutton. Some of the models wear cosmetics from Urban Decay. Have you heard of Urban Decay? Urban Decay eye shadow comes in colors such as "Bruise" and "Corpse." The nail polish comes in shades of "Mildew" and "Roach." Those who prefer diseases to wounds or insects can buy a tube of "Plague" lipstick instead.[2]

One New York fashion photographer explained the popularity of heroin chic as follows: "Designers look for inspiration to what's happening on the streets, and there are a lot of druggies everywhere."[3] The photographer is right. I have plenty of neighbors who are into heroin chic. I see them walking on South Street or gathering at picnic tables in the park around the corner. They do not smile and they wear black from head to toe, unless they have green hair or multi-colored tattoos.

Heroin chic is an act of rebellion. Its appeal is its "againstness," the way it stands over against conventional standards of color, dress, personality, grooming, and health. Calvin Klein says that his models are not supposed to be pretty. He describes them as "antiglamorous," which is just a fancy way of saying they are ugly. Heroin chic says, "If your colors are bright then I will wear black. If your smile is wide then I will scowl. If your body is strong then I will be sickly and wan. If your skin is smooth then I will pierce myself with angular metal. If you are beautiful then I will be ugly."

Not surprisingly, heroin chic has generated controversy in the fashion industry. Critics charge that it glamorizes drug use. It is irresponsible, they say, to encourage young people to look, dress, act, and even smell like junkies.

My purpose is not to criticize heroin chic, although you can probably guess that my tastes are rather different. Instead, I am interested in what heroin chic says about the human condition. Clothes cover the body, but they also have a way of uncovering the soul. What heroin chic uncovers is the ugliness of humanity. It tells us that the human soul is vacant, dark, gloomy, and unhappy.

This means that heroin chic tells the truth; not the whole truth, but the truth about what life is like apart from God. Fallen humanity *is* ugly. Sin blackens and wastes the human spirit. Our souls are punctured by the transgressions of our neighbors. Heroin chic is one way of honestly facing up to the realities of life without God. If there is no God, then cover me in black and hand me a tube of "Plague."

But heroin chic is only half of the truth. The other half begins with something we do not talk about often enough: the beauty of God. Psalm 27:4 says that the believer's greatest desire is "to gaze upon the beauty of the LORD." We learn from this verse that God is beauteous. Along with all of his other attributes—his goodness, truth, holiness, justice, and love—God is beautiful.

God is not only beautiful himself but he also loves beauty. "He has made everything beautiful in its time" (Eccl. 3:11). We can see it in the way he has made the world, and especially in the way he has made men and women. Human bodies are made in the image and likeness of God (Gen. 1:26). Among other things, this means that our bodies share in the beauty of God. They are invested with a permanent beauty, a beauty that outlasts even our fall into sin.

We are beautiful now and we will become even more beautiful in days to come. The prophet Zechariah imagined what we will look like on the day when the Lord comes again:

> The LORD their God will save them on that day. . . .
> They will sparkle in his land
>   like jewels in a crown.
> How attractive and beautiful they will be! (Zech. 9:16-17)

If God made us to be beautiful, then we are not to make ourselves ugly. Our bodies are not to be disfigured or mutilated. On the other hand, neither do they need to be glamorized or adorned unnecessarily. They are beautiful as they are.

So what should Christians wear? Christians can wear (almost) anything. And they can wear any color they please, because Jesus Christ is Lord of the spectrum. But whatever they wear, Christians wear it with modesty and dignity, to the glory of God. And they wear their clothes with a sense of beauty, because they serve a beautiful God.

# Part Five

# POLITICS

*If Christ is really king, exercising original and immediate jurisdiction over the State as really as he does over the Church, it follows necessarily that the general denial or neglect of his rightful lordship— any prevalent refusal to obey that Bible which is the open law-book of his kingdom—must be followed by political and social as well as moral and religious ruin. If professing Christians are unfaithful to the authority of their Lord in their capacity as citizens of the State, they cannot expect to be blessed by the indwelling of the Holy Ghost in their capacity as members of the Church. The kingdom of Christ is one, and cannot be divided in life or in death. If the Church languishes, the State cannot be in health.*

A. A. HODGE

THE AVERAGE AMERICAN SEEMS TO THINK that politics are the priority. What matters most is what is happening in Washington, which is why politics dominate the evening news.

Given this situation, it is not surprising that religion is only considered to be important when it affects politics. Political concerns are ultimate, and religious concerns become a matter of public significance only insofar as they have political implications. This explains why the evangelical church receives the most media attention during the campaign season or when Congress is considering legislation that deals with ethics or religion. It also explains the unprecedented coverage that Islam has received since the terrorist attack on the World Trade Center in New York. Religion is important for political reasons, not religious ones.

For most evangelical Christians, the situation is reversed. When they think about politics they think primarily in terms of its impact on religion. Which candidates have made a public testimony of faith in Jesus Christ? What kind of moral climate is the government creating for mercy ministry and evangelism? How will any proposed legislation affect the family or the church?

So who's right? Is religion important because of politics, or is politics important because of religion? The truth is that they both have their own significance and proper sphere of influence. Martin Luther taught that there are two kingdoms, the sacred and the secular, and that God rules over them both. Of course God is sovereign over the church, which he has put under the authority of Jesus Christ. But he is also sovereign over the secular state. As the Scripture says, "Everyone must submit himself to the governing authorities, for there is no authority except that which God has established. The authorities that exist have been established by God" (Rom. 13:1). The church is gathered by God's saving grace; the state is guided by his common grace; both are governed by his rule.

The essays in this section deal with issues that lie somewhere on the frontier between religion and politics. Not surprisingly, a number of them deal with 9/11 and its ongoing implications for America and the world. Many people seem to think that the spread of terrorism puts us in a new world situation. Perhaps it does, but the current conflict between Christianity and Islam is part of a struggle as ancient as the tension between politics and religion.

# 24

# HANG TEN?

The law of God has a way of offending people. People like Sally Flynn, for example. Ms. Flynn is the seventy-two-year-old atheist who filed suit against Chester County, Pennsylvania, seeking to have the Ten Commandments removed from the county courthouse.

The Ten Commandments have been hanging on the courthouse since before Sally Flynn was born. But Flynn thought it was time for the bronze plaque to come down. In a federal case called *Freethought Society of Greater Philadelphia v. Chester County,* she alleged that posting the Ten Commandments on a government building violated the United States Constitution. In her view, the plaque was an attempt to promote Christianity as the state religion, and thus contradicted the First Amendment. "Society knows about not murdering and not stealing," Flynn said, "but the rest of it there promotes a belief in God."

Flynn's suit was supported by the American Civil Liberties Union and by leaders from various religions. An imam testified that Muslims do not believe in the Ten Commandments. A rabbi said this particular plaque was offensive to Orthodox Jews because God's special divine name was transliterated from Hebrew into English. Others argued that the first commandment ("You shall have no other gods before me." Ex. 20:3) was offensive to Hindus and Buddhists because they believe in more than one deity.

In countering these arguments, Chester County officials appealed to the fact that the plaque has been in place for almost a century. To take it down now, they argued, would send the wrong message. The government is supposed to remain neutral where religion is concerned, but removing the Ten Commandments would show hostility rather than neutrality. The county also argued that although the Ten Commandments have a religious origin, they now have a "purely secular purpose." They have become so common in our society that they have lost their distinctively religious meaning. So posting them does not establish religion in any unconstitutional way.

The case was tried before United States District Court Judge Stuart Dalzell, who wasted little time in reaching his verdict. The day after closing arguments he ordered the county to take down the Ten Commandments. He wrote, "The only plaque on the courthouse façade with any substantive content is the Ten Commandment tablet. . . . [T]he tablet's necessary effect on those who see it is to endorse or advance the unique importance of this predominantly religious text for mainline Protestantism." And according to Mr. Dalzell at least, that makes it unconstitutional.

This verdict misunderstands the context in which our Constitution was written. The point of the establishment clause ("Congress shall make no law respecting an establishment of religion") was not to remove any mention of religion from public life, but to prevent the federal government from interfering with religion at the local level. At the time the Constitution was written, religion was already well established. Most states required Christian oaths not only for public officials, but also for citizens. Laws closely tied to the Ten Commandments, such as regulations governing blasphemy and the Sabbath, were common. To our founding fathers, the idea that posting the Ten Commandments might be unconstitutional would have seemed laughable. Yet now we are told that they pose a threat to religious freedom.

The county argued that the Ten Commandments are secular, not religious. Was this a good argument to make? Not from the legal standpoint, because the tablet was originally posted for an explicitly religious purpose. It was donated by the Council of Religious Education of the Federated Churches of West Chester to promote biblical teaching. Furthermore, in addition to the Ten Commandments, it also included the Two Great Commandments from the New Testament: "Love the Lord your God with all your heart" (Matt. 22:37) and "Love your neighbor as yourself" (Matt. 22:39). For the county to argue that such a plaque was not religious was to invite ridicule.

Nor was the county's argument valid from the religious standpoint. The law of God, as summarized in the Ten Commandments, has three primary uses. One is to restrain evil and promote virtue in civil society. This is its secular purpose, which the county was right to mention. Another use of the law is to expose our sin. The more we learn what God requires, the clearer it becomes that we are unable to do what he demands. This reveals our need for Jesus Christ. Once we come to Christ, the third use of the law is to show us how to live in a way that is pleasing to God.

So although the Ten Commandments have a secular purpose, they are inherently religious. By promoting the worship of only one God, by rejecting idolatry, and by regulating a weekly Sabbath, they promote biblical religion. It would have been wiser to admit this from the outset—certainly from the theological standpoint, and possibly also from the legal standpoint. Of course the Ten Commandments have a religious purpose! They always have, and they always will. But that does not prevent them from also having a secular benefit, and it does not make posting them unconstitutional.

Since we value the Ten Commandments and believe they have a salutary role to play in civic life, we lament their attempted removal from the Chester County Courthouse. For the same reason, we rejoice that Ms. Flynn's case was later overturned on appeal, and that the Ten Commandments have been restored to their rightful place on the building. Yet we continue to pray for the day when these laws will be written on our nation's heart.

# 25

# GOOD NEWS, BIBLE CLUBS

The Supreme Court of the United States passes judgment on many controversial issues surrounding the relationship between church and state. That was true again when the Court rendered its verdict in *Good News Club v. Milford Central School,* a case concerning the use of public school property for religious instruction during after-school hours.

The case arose in Milford, New York, where Stephen and Darleen Fournier sponsor a Good News Club for students ages six to twelve. The school district had adopted a policy for the use of its property by community groups. Any group that promoted "the moral and character development of children" was permitted to use school buildings for "instruction in any branch of education, learning or the arts."

In keeping with this policy—or so they thought—the Fourniers submitted a request to hold their Good News Club meetings in the cafeteria at Milford Central School. At these voluntary meetings, which would require parental approval, the Fourniers proposed to give children "a fun time of singing songs, hearing a Bible lesson and memorizing Scripture." The school board refused, however, claiming that the club's activities amounted to religious worship, which was excluded. According to district policy, school facilities could not be used "for the purpose of conducting religious instruction and Bible study."

What made the school board uneasy was the club's explicitly evangelistic purpose of "teaching children how to cultivate their relationship with God through Jesus Christ." Good News Clubs are part of a worldwide organization called Child Evangelism Fellowship. In keeping with its name, the purpose of a Good News Club is to share the gospel—the good news of salvation in Jesus Christ. This is valuable work because a child who is won for Christ has a whole lifetime to spend in the service of God and an eternity to praise him afterward.

With this in mind, the Good News Club in Milford is unashamedly evangelistic. This is how they describe their meetings: "The Club opens its session with Ms. Fournier taking attendance. As she calls a child's name, if the child recites a Bible verse the child receives a treat. After attendance, the Club sings songs. Next Club members engage in games that involve, *inter alia,* learning Bible verses. Ms. Fournier then relates a Bible story and explains how it applies to Club members' lives. The Club closes with prayer. Finally, Ms. Fournier distributes treats and the Bible verses for memorization."

Presumably the school board was not opposed to taking attendance or handing out treats. However, they strongly objected to using public property to help children convert to Christ. This hostility was later echoed by Supreme Court Justice David Souter, who complained in his dissent that Good News Clubs invite "unsaved" children to receive Christ as their personal Savior.

The Fourniers sued the school district in 1997, claiming that the board's decision violated their freedom of speech. The case eventually ended up before the Supreme Court, where by a vote of 6–3, the justices overturned an earlier ruling and determined that Milford should allow the Good News Club to meet on school property. The decision, carefully written by Clarence Thomas, had two major findings:

1. "When Milford denied the Good News Club access to the school's limited public forum on the ground that the Club was religious in nature, it discriminated against the Club because of its religious viewpoint in violation of the Free Speech Clause of the First Amendment."

2. "Permitting the Club to meet on the school's premises would not have violated the Establishment Clause." Indeed, rather than seeing any danger that the Good News Club would lead to an unconstitutional establishment of religion, the Court recognized the potential danger that people "would perceive a hostility toward the religious viewpoint if the Club were excluded from the public forum."

*Good News Club v. Milford Central School* represents a victory for religious freedom in America. In an environment of increasing hostility to Christianity, the decision provides some protection. Milford was not allowed to discriminate against a group on the basis of its Christian viewpoint. As one analyst explained, "The court essentially said you can't use the fact that someone is religious as an excuse to treat them worse than somebody else."[1]

The victory, however, is a small one. It only affects the use of public school property during after-school hours. And this only matters if Christians are willing to exercise their freedom to evangelize. The Bible says, "Be very careful, then, how you live—not as unwise but as wise, making the most of every opportunity, because the days are evil" (Eph. 5:15–16). That is what the Fourniers have been doing. They have been making the most of their opportunity to share the gospel, wisely seeking the full protection of the laws of our country.

The Fourniers have set a good example for Christians in America. Since the days are evil, we must make the most of every opportunity to witness for Christ. Hosting an after-school Bible club is one way to do this, but it is not the only one. But however we carry out our own personal evangelism, we should realize that witnessing in a secular society calls for wisdom.

Sometimes it helps to know our rights, and also to know when to fight for them. It has often been observed that if we do not exercise our freedoms, we will lose them. The truth is, however, that a freedom that is not exercised has been lost already. Therefore, we should be bold to exercise our freedom to speak for Christ. Of all the freedoms that we cherish, this is the one we hold most dear. It would be a tragedy to lose it, or even worse, to have lost it already by our failure to use it.[2]

# 26

# A NOT-SO CHARITABLE CHOICE?

They finally noticed. Politicians finally recognized that the church is able to do something that government has rarely if ever been able to do, and that is to develop poverty and addiction recovery programs that actually work.

This explains why, during his first months in office, one of the main items on President George W. Bush's agenda was to promote Faith-Based Initiatives. The President's goal was to allow religious groups to receive federal funding for the vital social services they offer to the poor and needy. Toward that end, he established a new White House Office of Faith-based and Community Initiatives, headed by Philadelphia native and University of Pennsylvania professor John J. DiIulio.

Tax dollars already go to secular organizations to pay for after-school care, drug treatment counseling, hunger relief, and other programs. However, complex federal regulations generally inhibit religious organizations from getting funding for which they are otherwise eligible. The President's new office intends to help religious charities obtain billions of federal tax dollars by reducing regulatory obstacles to their participation. His overall plan also includes larger tax deductions for Americans who make regular contributions to charity.

The stated objective of the program was to combat poverty, addiction, and homelessness. In the words of President Bush, "This is one of the most important initiatives that my administration will implement. There are deep needs and real suffering in the shadow of America's affluence. We are called by conscience to respond."

The President's reasoning is sound: faith-based programs work. Although as yet no scientific study has proven their superiority, there is evidence that they are more effective than most federal programs, some of which hardly work at all. To cite just one example, Teen Challenge achieves a remarkable 80% cure rate for teenage drug addicts. The reason for this is that the ministry gives students a life-changing encounter with Jesus Christ, and then instructs them in biblical principles for Christian living. Ultimately, social problems are always spiritual problems, which means that they find their best and fullest solution through the power of God, who provides "everything we need for life and godliness" (2 Peter 1:3).

Predictably, the President's plan met with a good deal of opposition on the grounds that it violated the Constitutional separation of church and state. Apparently, some people think that in order to protect itself from the dangers of religion, the government must actively discriminate against Christian charities. Because of this challenge, White House officials tried to emphasize that federal dollars will not be used for evangelism. In the words of one spokesperson, "This will not be funding religion. It is not the religious aspect of what they do that is getting funding, it is the community service aspect. These are not going to be programs that preach religion, these are faith-based programs that help people improve their lives."

The problem, of course, is that preaching religion is exactly what makes faith-based programs so effective. If they are to continue to be effective, then they must have the freedom to proclaim Christ. If the state wants to capitalize on the church's success in providing social services— as well it should—then it must leave the religious basis for providing those services intact. In the case of Christian organizations, this means having the freedom to present Jesus Christ as the answer to life's deepest needs.

The danger is that public concern about the separation of church and state will force Christian charities to compromise their mission. Federal funding rarely comes without strings attached, and it is important for Christian organizations—especially churches—to be cautious. One possible solution might be to grant tax credits to citizens who make donations to approved programs. This way the federal government could support effective charitable work without making direct subsidies to religious organizations.

The situation is somewhat different for independent ministries than it is for churches, but it is still wise to be cautious. Money never comes without temptation. Faith-based ministries always seem to be short of funds, and sometimes we dream about all the things we could do, if only we had more money. This is why some Christian groups immediately mobilized to apply for federal funds. But in my experience, God's work never lacks for God's supply. However useful it may be, money is among the least important resources needed for spiritual work, and it is important not to let the promise of money get in the way of sound principles for ministry.

Another difficulty with Faith-Based Initiatives is that the government is unable and unwilling to discriminate between Christian and non-Christian agencies. This means that in addition to supporting Christ-centered organizations, federal tax dollars would also go to non-Christian charities like Islamic mosques and even cults such as the Rev. Sun Myung Moon's Unification Church.

Government-sponsored faith-based initiatives are a mixed blessing. It is wise for politicians to acknowledge the effectiveness of the church, and to seek to assist Christian charities any way they can. For their part, Christians should be quick to point out that when it comes to America's most difficult social problems, the state is unable to do what the church can do. President Bush's initiative really amounted to an admission of federal failure. However, Christians should be cautious about becoming the social service arm of the state. When the government offers to help, it is not always wise to accept.[1]

# 27

# ATTACK ON AMERICA

Americans have a deep sense of national sadness about the attacks of September 11, 2001. What words would be adequate to express our grief for those who are dead and missing, our anguish at the way their lives were taken, our shock over our sudden vulnerability, or our fury at the harm that evil men will bring? At the same time, how can we possibly convey our admiration for the heroism of ordinary citizens or our renewed passion for our freedoms as Americans?

In our sorrow, in our lingering melancholy, we seek a Christian perspective. What does it all mean? How does God want us to respond? What does he want us to think and how does he want us to feel?

If there is one thing the people of God need to hear and believe, it is this: Even when everything else falls down, God is still standing. Yes, even when everything comes crashing down to earth, we are still safe, because God cannot be moved.

That great truth is beautifully expressed in Psalm 46, which begins and ends by affirming the absolute safety of those who trust in God:

> God is our refuge and strength,
>     an ever-present help in trouble.

Therefore we will not fear, though the earth give way
    and the mountains fall into the heart of the sea,
though its waters roar and foam
    and the mountains quake with their surging.
There is a river whose streams make glad the city of God,
    the holy place where the Most High dwells.
God is within her, she will not fall;
    God will help her at break of day.
Nations are in uproar, kingdoms fall;
    he lifts his voice, the earth melts.
The LORD Almighty is with us;
The God of Jacob is our fortress.
Come and see the works of the LORD,
    the desolations he has brought on the earth.
He makes wars cease to the ends of the earth;
    he breaks the bow and shatters the spear,
    he burns the shields with fire.
"Be still, and know that I am God;
    I will be exalted among the nations,
    I will be exalted in the earth."
The LORD Almighty is with us;
    the God of Jacob is our fortress.

God is our refuge, our strength, our fortress. The reason this is so important is because our world is *not* safe. There are reminders of this all through the psalm. It speaks of storms and earthquakes, wars and other disasters. Sometimes it seems as if the whole world is collapsing right underneath our feet. But God is not moved. He is strong and secure. The way that Psalm 46 shows this is by comparing him to a strong city.

The psalm says something about the city of God that I suppose I have always known, but has never seemed so desperately important as it now seems in light of the terrorist attacks on America. It says that the city of God will not fall. Notice the way verse 5 begins: "God is within her, she will not fall" (Ps. 46:5).

I sometimes talk about God's city with my children. We have a song we like to sing before bed. It comes from the beginning of Psalm 48, and it goes like this:

Great is the LORD,
and greatly to be praised
In the city of our God,
in the mountain of his holiness
Beautiful for situation,
The joy of the whole earth,
Is Mount Zion on the sides of the north,
The city of the Great King.

Sometimes, as we lie down in the quiet stillness of the evening, we talk about God's city. I will say, "Do you know what Mount Zion means?" And one of the children will say, "It means heaven," or "It's the city of God." Then I will ask, "What do you think it will be like? How big is it? How high does it reach? Who will be there?" Before we're finished, I will remind them that the very best thing about the city is that God is there. It's his city. It's where he lives and rules. And this is why it will never fall. The city of God is as strong as God himself. It is absolutely impregnable.

So take courage. Remember that our Lord Jesus Christ has triumphed over death. In the coming days our lives ought to be characterized by a holy defiance, not simply because we are Americans, but because we are Christians. We are undaunted by evil. We recognize it, but we are not afraid of it. Rather than living in fear, we are called to do everything by faith, working as hard as we ever have worked for the glory of God. This is because we belong to an eternal city—a city with everlasting foundations, whose builder and maker is God.

God's city will never fall. Therefore, God's people are always safe in God's city. Surely this includes all the believers whose lives were lost on

September 11, 2001. Some of them must have suffered greatly in their last moments of life. We continue to mourn their loss, horrified by the way they fell blazing from the sky to the earth. But they have landed on their feet, and now they are beyond all suffering. Like us they are waiting for God to glorify himself, for him to be exalted in every nation on the earth, as he has promised.

# 28

# AFTER THE ATTACK

"Life will never be the same again." This is what many Americans said in the aftermath of the "Attack on America," the suicide hijackings that brought down four airplanes, two of the world's tallest buildings, and a large section of the Pentagon. The terrorist attack was the deadliest ever to take place on American soil, with thousands of Americans and others perishing.

The loss has touched us all with horror, rage, compassion, and a deep sadness. During our lingering time of national sorrow, there are three relationships some Christians have had trouble keeping straight. These are the relationship between our church and our nation, between divine judgment and human evil, and between forgiveness and justice.

First, we need to distinguish between our church and our nation. Christians ought to be patriotic. God has called us to be good citizens of this great nation. Therefore, it is appropriate for us to have a strong sense of solidarity with our fellow Americans, to mourn our common losses, and to praise our uncommon heroes.

However, we must never confuse our commitment to our country with our even more fundamental commitment to Christ and his church. In particular, it is a mistake to think that we have the kind of spiritual connection with other Americans that enables us all to worship together.

The public services held in Washington, Philadelphia, New York, and elsewhere were characterized by an unholy mixture of Christianity with Judaism, Islam, and the good old U. S. of A. To do this is to mistake our civil union for a spiritual unity that we do not share.

It is right and good for us to have public gatherings to show our love for our country, and also to express our grief for the loss we share. But this should not take place in the context of public worship. The result can only be a lack of clarity about the one true gospel. This is why our founding fathers advocated a separation between church and state—not because the church would corrupt our society, but because the true ministry of God's Word needs to be protected from the secular state.

As Christians, we also need to distinguish between divine judgment and human evil. Nearly everyone recognizes that the attacks were the actions of wicked men—"evildoers," as President George W. Bush called them. This means that God is not to blame. The terrorist attacks were not acts of God, but acts of men in rebellion against God. However, some Christians have been saying that God permitted these attacks in order to judge our country for its many sins. One well-known pastor said, "I really believe that the pagans, and the abortionists, and the feminists, and the gays and the lesbians who are actively trying to make that an alternative lifestyle, the ACLU, People For the American Way, all of them have tried to secularize America. I point the finger in their face and say 'you helped this happen.'" (The minister has since apologized, but he was not alone in his opinions.)

There are many problems with viewing terrorist activity as a form of divine judgment. One is that judgment begins with the house of God (1 Peter 4:17), so that if God intends to judge America, we can expect him to start with the American church. Besides, we have no way of knowing God's purpose. Was the attack intended to serve as a spiritual wake-up call? Was it God's way of punishing us for our greed? Who knows? God's purpose has not been revealed, and therefore it is useless for us to speculate.

One thing we can say for certain is that the tragedy calls us all to repentance. Consider the question that Jesus asked his disciples: "Those eighteen who died when the tower in Siloam fell on them—do you think they were more guilty than all the others living in Jerusalem? I tell you, no! But unless you repent, you too will all perish" (Luke 13:4–5). Jesus was talking about a calamity from his own time—the collapse of a great building, with the sudden loss of human life. His point was that people should stop trying to guess why God allowed such a tragedy. Our guesses are bound to be wrong anyway. What we ought to do instead is ponder our own relationship to God, and in the light of the coming judgment, to repent and not to perish.

The last thing Christians have trouble keeping straight is the relationship between justice and forgiveness. Most Americans were justifiably outraged by these acts of terror, and still desperately hope that everyone who conspired against our country will be brought to justice. In their zeal for retaliation, some Christians err on the side of vengeance. God says, "It is mine to avenge; I will repay" (Rom. 12:19), but frankly, some of us wouldn't mind getting in on the action. Instead, we must be content to wait for justice to be carried out by the authorities that God has established as agents of his wrath "to bring punishment" on those who do wrong (Rom. 13:4).

Other Christians oppose the very idea of seeking justice. They are quick to quote the words of Jesus, who said, "Love your enemies and pray for those who persecute you" (Matt. 5:44). Certainly it is good for us to pray for our personal enemies, and especially to ask God to save them by his grace. It is also important to forgive our enemies, so that we do not strike out in unholy rage. However, at the same time that we are praying for and (God help us!) forgiving our enemies, we must also seek to bring them to justice, especially if they have committed acts of public violence against innocent victims. There is no contradiction between forgiveness, which offers grace to those who sin, and justice, which brings their sin to account.

In the aftermath of the attack, as we wrestle with many profound spiritual questions, I am reminded of a letter Dorothy L. Sayers wrote to a friend who had experienced great suffering, and wanted to know

"Why does everything go wrong?" and "What is the meaning of all this suffering?" When Sayers wrote back, she was able to answer both questions in only three words. Why does everything go wrong? "Sin." What is the meaning of all this suffering? "Christ crucified." The reason there is such great trouble in the world is because of the terrible things that people do to one another. But there is real meaning in all this suffering, because the very Son of God has entered into it and ultimately redeemed it through his own sufferings and death on the cross.

# 29

# FREEDOM OF RELIGION

In the wake of the September 11 terrorist attacks on New York and Washington, President Bush and other leaders took great pains to assure the world that Islam is a peace-loving religion. People were told that America is a place where Christians, Jews, and Muslims can walk hand in hand. Undoubtedly this was good politics. It helped to reassure the leaders of Muslim nations that we were not at war with them, or their religion, but only with an evil and violent network of terrorists.

What is less clear is whether affirming Islam makes for good religion. Notwithstanding all the recent claims that Islam is a peace-loving religion, the Koran itself teaches that unbelievers should be put to death. "Fight against such of those who have been given the Scripture as believe not in Allah," the Koran says (Surah 9:29). "Allah will afflict [unbelievers] with a doom from Him at our hands" (Surah 9:52). Islam is a fundamentally intolerant faith.

In light of the current confusions about Islam and with all of the current turmoil in politics and world religion, it is important to remember what Christianity teaches about the freedom of religion.

In the *Charter of Privileges* that he wrote on October 28, 1701, William Penn argued that "no people can be truly happy though under the Greatest Enjoyments of Civil Liberties if Abridged of the Freedom of their Consciences as to their Religious Profession and worship." In other words, all our other freedoms will become meaningless if we lose the freedom of religion.

With this danger in mind, Penn went on to make the following declaration:

> I do hereby Grant and Declare that no person or persons Inhabiting in this Province or Territories who shall Confess and Acknowledge one Almighty God the Creator upholder and Ruler of the world and profess him or themselves Obliged to live quietly under the Civil Government shall be in any case molested or prejudiced in his or their person or Estate because of his or their Conscientious persuasion or practice nor be compelled to frequent or maintain any Religious Worship place or Ministry contrary to his or their mind or do or Suffer any other act or thing contrary to their Religious persuasion [some spelling has been modernized].

To put all of this more simply, citizens cannot be discriminated against on the basis of their religion; nor can they be coerced into practicing a religion that they do not wish to claim as their own. America has been a land of religious liberty ever since.

William Penn's interest in the freedom of religion partly arose out of his own experience. He had been imprisoned in the Tower of London for his Quaker beliefs. Indeed, it was while he was locked up in the Tower that he developed his plan for a free society protecting the freedom of the conscience.

Religious liberty has always been part of what it means to be a good Pennsylvanian. It is also part of what it means to be a good Presbyterian. Even before William Penn, English and Scottish Presbyterians argued for the necessity of religious liberty. Indeed, Penn's convictions on the subject came from his study of Reformed theologians such as John Owen. In our own Westminster Confession of Faith (23.3) we read that:

It is the duty of civil magistrates to protect the Church of our common Lord, without giving the preference to any denomination of Christians above the rest. . . . And, as Jesus Christ hath appointed a regular government and discipline in his Church, no law of any commonwealth should interfere with, or hinder, the due exercise thereof, among the voluntary members of *any* denomination of Christians, according to their own profession and belief. It is the duty of civil magistrates to protect the person and good name of all their people, in such an effectual manner as that no person be suffered, either upon pretense of religion or of infidelity, to offer any indignity, violence, abuse, or injury to any other person whatsoever. . . . (emphasis added)

Why is religious liberty so important to us as Christians? In part, it is because we cherish our freedom to assemble for public worship and to proclaim the good news about Jesus Christ. We would do these things anyway, of course, but it is one of our great privileges as citizens of the United States to worship and witness under the full protection of the law.

But why are we in favor of extending the same freedom to others, including people of other faiths, or even people who do not claim to be religious at all? It is because we believe in the power of God. We believe that the Holy Spirit, speaking in Scripture, has the power to save sinners, and this change is an inward transformation that cannot be outwardly coerced. As long as we have the freedom to teach what the Bible says about the person and work of Jesus Christ, then even if other people have the freedom to share other faiths, we know that God will do his saving work through his gospel. All we ask is the freedom of our religion.

Fifty years after William Penn signed his famous *Charter,* the City of Philadelphia commemorated the occasion by commissioning a bell. In the Old Testament, the fiftieth year is the Jubilee—a year of liberty. Mindful of that fact, the citizens of Philadelphia engraved the bell with a text from Leviticus: "Proclaim liberty throughout all the land unto all the inhabitants thereof" (Lev. 25:10 KJV). By the command of Almighty God, this is still our duty today: to proclaim liberty in Christ throughout the land. By God's grace it is not only our duty, but also our freedom. May it ever remain so.

# 30

# DOES GOD TAKE SIDES?

Does God take sides? Roger Rosenblatt doesn't think so. In an essay in the December 17, 2001 issue of *Time* magazine, Rosenblatt asked which side of the war against terrorism God is on. Is he on our side, as so many Americans assume, or is he on the side of al-Qaeda?

Roger Rosenblatt doesn't think that God is on anyone's side at all. As the title of his essay reads, "God Is Not on My Side. Or Yours." "One would like to think that God is on our side against the terrorists," writes Rosenblatt, "because the terrorists are wrong and we are in the right, and any deity worth his salt would be able to discern that objective truth. But this is simply good-hearted arrogance cloaked in morality—the same kind of thinking that makes people decide that God created humans in his own image."

According to Mr. Rosenblatt, the reason that God is not on anyone's side in particular is that God just isn't that interested in what is happening in the world. Rosenblatt writes:

> I would like to offer the opinion that God is not thinking about us.
> Or if he is, one has no way of knowing that—unless, of course, one
> is like Mohamed Atta, who had a pathological view of faith, or Jerry

Falwell, whose mind is Taliban minus the bloodlust. This week the Taliban leader, Mohammed Omar, may be wondering how tight he is with God, after all. In September he was certain that God rooted for our extinction. Now, with the surrender of Kandahar, the mullah may be shopping for a more competent deity.

Sadly, this is the kind of journalism that Bible-believing Christians have come to expect from the secular media. Despite the fact that it is biblically ill-informed, it presumes to theologize in front of a national audience. It also resorts to making facile comparisons between fundamental Christians and hardened terrorists. The comment about Jerry Falwell is a cheap shot. Still, the question that Rosenblatt raises is worth considering: Assuming that he is even interested enough to care, does God take sides?

The Bible teaches that God does take sides. Certainly he takes sides when it comes to salvation. The Bible says, "The LORD watches over the way of the righteous, but the way of the wicked will perish" (Ps. 1:6). Everywhere the Bible discriminates between the elect and the reprobate, the saved and the lost, the sheep and the goats, the redeemed and the damned.

God also takes sides in the great affairs of men and nations. The Bible teaches that God "rules over the nations" (Ps. 22:28), that he "foils the plans of the nations" (Ps. 33:10), that he "reigns over the nations" (Ps. 47:8), that he "disciplines nations" (Ps. 94:10), and that he will "judge the nations" (Ps. 110:6). However—and this is a crucial qualification—although God blesses the righteous and punishes the wicked, he almost never does it immediately. In fact, justice will not be fully served until the Day of Judgment.

This delay makes it difficult, if not impossible, to use current events to figure out whose side God is on. Here Mr. Rosenblatt has a point: It is presumptuous for us to claim that we know exactly what God is doing, that we know who he is for and who he is against. However, and this is the problem with Mr. Rosenblatt's argument, it is one thing to say that we don't always know whose side God is on, and another thing to say that he doesn't take sides at all. Clearly, God *does* take sides, for the Scripture says, "If God is for us, who can be against us?" (Rom. 8:31).

It is important to understand that when it comes to taking sides, God thinks primarily in spiritual terms, not military or political terms. No nation in the world—including the United States of America—can claim God's unqualified blessing. God is for his people, but his people are scattered among all the nations of the world, united by faith in Christ.

No doubt Mr. Rosenblatt would object to my saying that God is on our side. He objects to the idea that God "micromanages the universe for the advantage of particular believers." But this objection is based on a misunderstanding. God's purpose is not to make the universe work for our advantage, but to glorify himself. Often God achieves this by bringing his people through suffering and hardship rather than by making things work out to their obvious advantage. When we say that God takes sides, we do not mean that things always go well for his people, but that no matter how things go, he is glorified by their faith and obedience.

Then there is this to consider: As he carries out his plan of salvation, God is busy turning some of his enemies into friends. The gospel is a message of reconciliation. This is why it is impossible say that God is against any particular individual. Is God against evil? Yes. Is he opposed to acts of terror, such as those committed last September? Always. Does he take sides against an organization like al-Qaeda? Of course. Is he against the followers of Osama bin Laden? Certainly he hates what they have done, but it is at least possible that some of them are destined to receive salvation. If so, then God is *for* them, not against them, and ultimately he will bring them to repent of their sins and believe in Jesus Christ.

Even if God is for me, that doesn't mean that everything I do necessarily has his endorsement. This is a mistake Christians often make, and it is easy to understand why someone like Roger Rosenblatt gets nervous when people start claiming that God is on their side. In my view, America's intervention in Afghanistan is necessary and just, and in that sense, God is on our side. This does not mean, however, that our soldiers are without sin, or even that our campaign against terrorism will be a success. What we do know is that whatever happens, it will be for the ultimate good of God's people, and for the glory of our God.

# Part Six

# FEASTS AND FESTIVALS

*Our society has forgotten how to celebrate. It has associated celebration with dissipation. It has turned the festival of the birth of Christ into a gluttonous spending spree and the festival of the resurrection of Christ into a spring egg-roll and candy-hunt. These occasions now nurture in children not a sense of the holy God, but a selfish desire to possess. Such acquisitiveness can never lead to true celebration, for the latter is inherently turned outward. We cannot celebrate ourselves; we can only celebrate others. As friends and relatives mark the passing of another year, we celebrate the gift of their birth. As we prepare for the holy days, we ready our hearts and spirits for the thanksgiving and praise of the occasion—so that we can celebrate God's gifts of himself and his grace.*

MARVA DAWN

WE WERE MADE TO GLORIFY GOD and enjoy him forever. Or to put it another way, we were made to celebrate.

God's people have always gathered for sacred festivals. In the Old Testament the Israelites assembled in Jerusalem for three pilgrim feasts: Passover, Weeks, and Tabernacles. Israel's worship year was organized around these holy festivals, as well as around the weekly celebration of the Sabbath. Similarly, in the New Testament we often find Jesus sitting down to feast with his disciples. In fact, this formed the basis for one common criticism against him: he spent too much time celebrating, and with the wrong crowd. This was all in preparation for the party to end all parties—"the wedding supper of the Lamb" (Rev. 19:9).

God is not a spoilsport. On the contrary, he has made us for the joy of feasts and festivals. It is inevitable, then, that when people turn away from God, they still want to party. It is in our nature. This helps to explain why Americans celebrate a growing number of secular holidays, like Halloween, which has become a major event on the annual calendar. We were made to celebrate, and if we do not celebrate God, we still have to celebrate something.

What is different about most contemporary celebrations, of course, is that they no longer have God at the center. Even Christian holidays like Christmas have lost most of their sacred significance. People still want to celebrate, but they would just as soon leave God out of it. Then the only purpose left is to have a good time, but the real joy of feasting—which is to praise God for his goodness and grace—has vanished.

The following essays deal with several common holidays in our culture, including one that may come as a surprise. They are offered in the hope that we will not forget what it means to feast to the glory of God, with all the good humor and great fun that come from his grace.

# 31

# APRIL FOOL!

True story. According to the October 30, 2000, edition of the *Chicago Sun Times*, a pig traveled on a six-hour US Airways flight from Philadelphia to Seattle. And he didn't ride coach, either. Two passengers convinced an airline representative that the pig was a "therapeutic companion pet"—sort of like a seeing-eye dog—so the pig was permitted to sit with them in the first-class cabin of the airplane.

Passengers variously described the 300-pound animal as "enormous, brown, angry, and honking." The pig was seated with his companions in three seats near the front of the plane. However, flight attendants reportedly had difficulty strapping him in. According to eyewitnesses, the pig "became restless after takeoff and sauntered through the cabin." One passenger complained, "He kept rubbing his nose on people's legs trying to get them to give him food."

Upon landing, things only got worse. To quote the *Sun Times*, "The pig panicked, running up and down through economy class squealing." Many passengers—also screaming—stood on their seats. It took four attendants to escort the pig out of the airplane; upon reaching the terminal, he escaped, although he was later recaptured. When asked to comment on the story, US Airways spokesman David Castelveter said,

"We can confirm that the pig traveled, and we can confirm that it will never happen again."

As I say, this is a true story. It is also a funny story, but what makes it funny? I think the answer is at least partly theological. Although it is always more entertaining to laugh at jokes than to explain them, there is a place for giving a short theology of humor.

First, there is some humor in creation. Think of the animals that God has made. There is something inherently comical about a pig, for example, whether or not he happens to be a frequent flyer. The humorous antics of the animals reveal the playfulness of God—his smile on all creation.

Second, a great deal of humor arises from the tragedy of fallen humanity. We were made in the very image of God (Gen. 1:27). Yet we have fallen from innocence, and there is something inherently comical, not to say ridiculous, about a creature of such obvious dignity making mistakes, moral and otherwise. This explains why a pig on an airplane is so much funnier than, say, a pig in a pigsty. Deep down, we know that we were made for something better, and yet we are always struggling with our limitations. Some of the best humor arises from the gap between our dignity and our fallibility.

What enables us to laugh at ourselves, however, is the possibility of redemption. This is a third principle for a short theology of humor. If we were beyond the reach of grace, life would be nothing to laugh about. But we live in a world where God pulled off the biggest practical joke ever, gaining victory out of apparent defeat by bringing Jesus back from the dead. It is the promise of redemption in Christ that keeps us from despair, and thus enables us to laugh through our tears.

The *Philadelphia Inquirer* once ran a story about an art show sponsored by a church in Camden, New Jersey. The exhibit featured images of Jesus, especially of his face. The article was accompanied by several pictures, including—to my amazement—one of Jesus laughing. I cannot ever remember seeing a picture of Jesus laughing. Smiling perhaps, with gentle warmth, but never laughing. Yet surely what the artist drew is theologically correct. If Jesus really is a man, as the Bible says he is, then he must be able to enjoy a good joke as much as the next guy. Maybe even better, because he knows how it will all turn out in the end. It was Jesus who promised his disciples that they would have the last laugh. "Blessed are you who weep now," he said, "for you will laugh" (Luke 6:21; cf. Job 8:21; Ps. 126:2).

Not all laughter is redemptive, of course. Some humor comes from the unregenerate nature. There is vulgarity, what the Bible calls "coarse jesting" (Eph. 5:4 NKJV). There is gallows humor, the kind workers resort to before the next round of layoffs. A friend once told me that the joke going around his office was that they were going to take up a collection to send their manager to the Wharton School to learn how to run a business. Then there is sarcasm, the cutting remark that uses cruelty to produce comedy.

These forms of humor are not redemptive. People who tell such jokes are really jeering at God, having a laugh at his expense. Dirty jokes are a way of saying that what God has made is unclean, and therefore worthy of derision. Sarcasm and other forms of dark humor also steal a laugh—in this case at the expense of someone made in God's image. Sadly, the jokes that get the loudest laughs (and thus the jokes that people tell most often) fall into these sinful categories. It shows that we are depraved right down to the funny bone. If that is true, then we need God to sanctify our sense of humor as much as we need him to sanctify everything else.

I once saw a bumper sticker plastered to the back of a parking sign. It read, "National Atheist's Day," and the date given was "April 1st." The small print contained the following Bible verse: "The fool says in his heart, 'There is no God' " (Ps. 53:1). I could appreciate the humor in the bumper sticker, but I'm not sure I agreed with its theology. I rather think that April 1st belongs to believers, for we serve the God of laughter.

## 32

# TRICK OR TREAT?

America's second most popular holiday, Halloween, often poses a dilemma for Christian families. On the one hand, we are not opposed to carving pumpkins, dressing up in costumes, visiting our neighbors, or sharing our candy. In fact, we are positively in favor of all those things. On the other hand, we *are* opposed to ghouls, ghosts, and goblins. Hence our dilemma. Halloween is a dangerous mixture of good, wholesome fun and dark, deceptive evil.

Halloween has its origins in the druid festivals of the ancient Celts. The druids were pagan priests. According to the Celtic calendar, October 31 was the last day of the year, known as "Samhain," or "summer's end." The druids marked the passing of the old year by celebrating death. First they gathered food for their festivities, which may have been the origin of "trick-or-treating." Then they gathered around huge bonfires at which they held sinister rituals, sacrificing animals and even human beings to appease their gods. These sacrifices were intended to free the souls of the dead from their bondage. Ultimately, of course, the druids were worshipping Satan.

Some of these practices continued even after the Christianization of Europe. The word "Halloween" is derived from the phrase "All Hallow's Eve." For early medieval Christians, November 1 was All Hallow's Day, or All Saint's Day. It was a day for remembering the saints of the past, especially Christians who had died during the previous year. If November 1 was All Hallow's Day, then October 31 was All Hallow's Eve, or "Hallowe'en." Since the church never quite managed to drive paganism out of Europe, Halloween remained a night for reveling in evil.

Halloween is sometimes called "the Devil's birthday." This is not true, of course. Satan was created before this world began, and he has no right to claim October 31 for his own. Jesus Christ is Lord of the calendar. Halloween, like every day, is a day that the Lord has made—"let us rejoice and be glad in it" (Ps. 118:24). But even if the devil does not have a birthday, Halloween probably *is* his favorite night of the year. It is the night when witches gather in their covens to swear his allegiance and to recite incantations against the church. It is the night when people venture into the haunting darkness, dressed up as frightful monsters.

The biggest danger with Halloween is the way that it trivializes evil. Children, especially, are led to believe that wizards and witches are fun, in a spooky kind of way. This is one of Satan's favorite tricks: Getting people to think that evil is a treat.

We live in a culture where Satanic influences are accepted as part of daily life. In the streets of Philadelphia there are spirit shops. On our television sets there are situation comedies featuring the practical magic of seductive young witches. In the schoolyard, children are trading Pokémon cards to gain new powers. Some of them will take the next step and graduate to "Magic: the Gathering," a sort of advanced form of Pokémon that is really an introduction to the occult. At the bookstores they are selling millions of copies of Harry Potter, a series of books set at Hogwarts School of Witchcraft and Wizardry. On our nation's military bases, the Wiccans have been granted the freedom to assemble for Satanic rituals. Halloween has its part to play in all this neo-paganism. For many it is the first step on a path that leads deeper and deeper into the bewitching darkness.

The Bible contains many strong warnings against having anything to do with witchcraft of any kind. This is what God said, through his prophet Moses: "Let no one be found among you who . . . practices divination or sorcery, interprets omens, engages in witchcraft, or casts spells, or who is a medium or spiritist who consults the dead. Anyone who does these things is detestable to the LORD. . . . But as for you, the LORD your God has not permitted you to do so. The LORD your God will raise up for you a prophet like me from among your own brothers. You must listen to him" (Deut. 18:10–12a, 14b–15). When Moses spoke of a prophet like himself, a prophet worth listening to, he was ultimately referring to Jesus Christ (cf. Matt. 17:5). He was saying that we have to choose whom we will listen to. Either we can listen to witches and wizards, or we can listen to God's own Son, but we cannot listen to both.

In some respects, Halloween is an area where individual Christians have some freedom to determine what it means to be in the world without being of the world. Some Christian parents refuse to let their children have anything whatsoever to do with Halloween. Others may allow them to wear costumes to school or around the neighborhood. Perhaps there is some wisdom in Christians having alternative events of their own, like throwing a Noah's Ark party, or celebrating Reformation Day on the last Sunday in October, or remembering the dearly departed saints on November 1 (although even such practices can become superstitious).

But there can be no compromise when it comes to any form of witchcraft, which the New Testament describes as an "act of the sinful nature" which prevents its practitioners from inheriting the kingdom of God (Gal. 5:19–21). With so many demonic images around at Halloween, Christian parents should warn their children about the dangers of becoming enchanted by evil. I think of a toddler who arrived at preschool, only to find his teacher dressed as a witch. "It's scary, Mommy!" he said. The little boy was not about to be tricked by one of Satan's "treats." Neither should we. On Halloween, as on every night, Christians should pray that God would deliver us from the Evil One (Matt. 6:13).

# 33

# THE *REAL* "TWELVE DAYS OF CHRISTMAS"?

A missionary agency once sent me a newsletter explaining the real meaning of "The Twelve Days of Christmas"—or so I thought. But first, a little background: The traditional twelve days of Christmas are not the days before Christmas, but the days after. They end on January 6, the Day of Epiphany, traditionally considered to be the day that the Magi brought their gifts to the Christ child (see Matt. 2:1–12). In some places it is customary to exchange gifts, not only on Christmas, but also on Epiphany, and each day in between. Hence the well-known song: "On the first day of Christmas, my true love gave to me, a partridge in a pear tree," and so forth.

According to the literature I received, there is a code to unlock the meaning of the popular song. The newsletter began by stating that "Christians were forbidden to teach Scripture outside of the established church in sixteenth-century England. So they developed creative ways to conceal Bible truths in songs. The Christmas song 'The Twelve Days of Christmas' is an example of this teaching method. Each day's gift symbolizes a Christian teaching." In other words, the popular carol is not a silly love song after all, but a sort of underground musical catechism for preserving Christian doctrine. The "true love" turns out to be God himself, the giver of every good gift.

The newsletter went on to explain the meaning of each gift (based on a 1997 book by Helen Haidle called *The Story Behind the Song: The Real 12 Days of Christmas*). To begin with, "The partridge is an ancient Christian symbol of Christ; a small but valiant bird known for its willingness to die to save its young. The pear tree represents the cross." Next come two turtledoves, a reminder of the sacrifice that Mary and Joseph offered when they dedicated Jesus at the Temple (Luke 2:24). French hens were costly in the sixteenth century; they represent the precious gifts of faith, hope, and love (1 Cor. 13:13), or perhaps the three gifts of the Wise Men. The four calling birds bespeak the four Gospels— Matthew, Mark, Luke, and John. Five golden rings represent God's eternity. And so it goes: six geese for six days of creation; seven swans for seven gifts of the Holy Spirit; eight maids for eight Beatitudes; nine ladies for the fruit of the Spirit; ten lords for the Ten Commandments; eleven pipers for eleven faithful disciples; and twelve drummers for the dozen articles of the Apostles' Creed.

Now that is a fascinating explanation of "The Twelve Days of Christmas." However, I was curious about the song's exact origins, so I decided to do a little more research, by way of the Internet. The more I looked, the more suspicious I became, as I discovered several things that didn't quite add up.

For one thing, I kept getting conflicting information about what each day meant. Some sources indicated that the turtledoves stood for the Old and New Testaments; that the three French hens represented the Father, the Son, and the Holy Ghost; that the five golden rings were the Five Books of Moses; or that the seven swans were the seven sacraments of the Roman Catholic church. It was beginning to seem like the song meant whatever you wanted it to mean.

Also, most of the articles claimed that the song was written for the benefit of young English Catholics who hoped to learn the basics of their faith without getting persecuted. However, there is nothing in the song that is distinctively Catholic. (The only possible exception is the seven sacraments, if that is the meaning of "seven swans a-swimming.") The gifts in "The Twelve Days of Christmas" are ones that any Protestant would be happy to receive, such as the Gospels or the fruit of the Spirit. There could hardly have been a need for Catholics to develop a code song for such widely accepted biblical facts as the Ten Commandments. Besides, the song really does not work as a memory aid because it contains hardly any information. For example, the phrase "eight maids a-milking" is not very helpful for actually remembering all eight of the Beatitudes.

In the course of my research, I began to notice that many of the articles used similar phrases and sentences. Frankly, some of them were plagiarized, and they could all be traced to a single source: an article written by Father Hal Stockert and posted on the "Catholic Information Network." Apparently, Father Stockert was the first to claim that "The Twelve Days of Christmas" was a musical code. He makes this claim on the basis of his own research in historical documents, such as seventeeth-century letters. Unfortunately, he also admits that his original notes were lost in a flood, which leaves his interpretation completely unsubstantiated.

Finally, I arrived at a website called "Urban Legends," sponsored by the San Fernando Valley Folklore Society. After examining the evidence, the Folklore Society reaches what is undoubtedly the safest conclusion: The idea that "The Twelve Days of Christmas" is a code that Roman Catholics developed to escape persecution is at best unverified, and at worst completely false.

There are some lessons to learn from my quest. One is not to believe everything you read, especially on the Internet. Another is how easy it is for rumors to spread. But perhaps the most important lesson is that a tradition is only as valid as the facts behind it. This is especially important to remember at Christmas, when legends abound—legends about snowmen and reindeer, about poinsettias and Santa Claus. There are even legends about the birth of Christ, such as the little drummer boy, or "little Lord Jesus no crying he makes."

But Christmas itself is no legend. It is based on the fact that God sent his Son Jesus Christ to be our Savior. Jesus came to live the perfect life that we could never live, to die the painful death that we deserved to die, and to enter the glorious heaven that we hope to enter. It all began in Bethlehem, where Mary "gave birth to her firstborn, a son . . . wrapped him in cloths and placed him in a manger, because there was no room for them in the inn" (Luke 2:7).

# 34

# STAR OF BETHLEHEM

*The star was so beautiful, large, and clear,*
*That all the other stars of the sky*
*Became a white mist in the atmosphere.*
*And by this they knew that the coming was near*
*Of the Prince foretold in prophecy.*

Thus wrote Henry Wadsworth Longfellow concerning the Star of Bethlehem, which of all the signs and wonders surrounding the first Christmas is perhaps the most mysterious.

The Bible says that some time after Jesus was born, "Magi from the east came to Jerusalem and asked, 'Where is the one who has been born king of the Jews? We saw his star in the east and have come to worship him'" (Matt. 2:1–2). The Magi obviously had an interest in astronomy. Probably they were astrologers, men who consulted the stars to make predictions about what was happening in the world. As they studied the heavens, they saw something to indicate that a king had been born in Judea, but what, exactly, did they see?

There have been many theories. Some Christians think that the star was a supernatural light—something never seen before, or since. They imagine it hovering over the Magi on their journey, directly guiding them until finally coming to rest a few feet over the house where Jesus was. Others think it was a comet or a conjunction of planets. Johannes Kepler thought it was a supernova—an exploding star. Still others think it was a meteor shower. The noted British astronomer Sir Patrick Moore published a book arguing that the bright light that identified the birthplace of Christ could only have been caused by shooting stars.[1]

What are we to make of this and other theories? The place to start is with the biblical facts. First there is the word "star," which seems straightforward enough. However, the Greek word does not settle the matter because it can also refer to other heavenly objects.

The next fact to notice is that the Star of Bethlehem made a sudden appearance. The Wise Men saw it rising in the east (Matt. 2:2). Presumably they had never seen anything like it. Otherwise, why would they have followed it? The star's sudden emergence is confirmed by King Herod, who "called the Magi secretly and found out from them the exact time the star had appeared" (Matt. 2:7).

The star disappeared just as suddenly as it appeared. This is why the Magi stopped in Jerusalem to ask for directions instead of going straight to Bethlehem. Then the star *re*appeared! This is the clear implication of verses 9 and 10: "After they had heard the king, they went on their way, and the star they had seen in the east went ahead of them until it stopped over the place where the child was. When they saw the star, they were overjoyed."

It is of course possible that the Magi saw some supernatural light that God kept bringing in and out of the sky as needed. However, in that case one would expect other people to have seen it and perhaps even to have followed it. The trouble is that there is no record of any such celestial event during the appropriate time period. Nor are there any records of comets or novas. In all probability the Star of Bethlehem was a subtler sign, the kind of thing that only experts like the Magi would have even noticed.

The most convincing explanation is that they witnessed several conjunctions of Jupiter, the planet they considered to represent kingship. A number of such conjunctions took place in the years leading up to the death of Herod. In its annual program "Star of Wonder," Chicago's Adler Planetarium makes a persuasive case for one of these celestial events. This view is also advocated by Craig Chester of the Monterey Institute for Research in Astronomy, who writes,

> In September of 3 B.C., Jupiter came into conjunction with Regulus, the star of kingship, the brightest star in the constellation of Leo. Leo was the constellation of kings, and it was associated with the Lion of Judah. The royal planet approached the royal star in the royal constellation representing Israel. Just a month earlier, Jupiter and Venus, the Mother planet, had almost seemed to touch each other in another close conjunction, also in Leo. Then the conjunction between Jupiter and Regulus was repeated, not once but twice, in February and May of 2 B.C. Finally, in June of 2 B.C., Jupiter and Venus, the two brightest objects in the sky save the sun and the moon, experienced an even closer encounter when their disks appeared to touch; to the naked eye they became a single object above the setting sun. This exceptionally rare spectacle could not have been missed by the Magi.[2]

When the Magi saw this "star," they headed for Jerusalem. The Bible does not say that they followed the star at this point in their journey, but only that they went to Judea. However, they did follow the star to Bethlehem. They would have seen Jupiter and Venus in the south, and followed it the five miles to Bethlehem. When they reached the village they would have seen it above the horizon—from their perspective stopping over the place where the child was.

If one of these astronomical events involving Jupiter is the right interpretation, it is a remarkable testimony to God's sovereignty. It means that from the very creation of the world, God organized the solar system—and indeed the entire universe—in a way that would signify the birth of his Son and our Savior, Jesus Christ.

It is also a remarkable testimony to God's grace. How strange it is that the Savior's birth was first revealed to *astrologers*. God had always forbidden astrology. Nevertheless, he used a heavenly sign to lead the Magi to Jesus. This does not mean that God condones horoscopes. It does mean that he speaks to people where they are, in ways that they can understand, in order ultimately to lead them to himself. The Magi did not know anything about Jesus when they first set out for Judea. But they followed the one clue that God gave them, and in the end they met him as their Savior and Lord.

Jesus said, "He who seeks finds" (Matt. 7:8). This is still true today. Everyone who truly seeks after God will find him. God is not likely to send a star, or even a planetary conjunction. But he has given plenty of clues in his creation, and even more clues in his Word. Anyone who is wise will seek him, and anyone who seeks him will find him.

# 35

# GIFT EXCHANGE

I enjoy giving Christmas presents almost as much as I enjoy getting them. However, I don't always enjoy shopping for them and I'm always glad when I'm finished. Generally I make a run to Barnes & Noble; I come from a literary family. Then we have a big family outing—Toys R Us, Zany Brainy, and the mall—looking for gifts for the cousins. With marvelous efficiency, my wife wraps all the presents and boxes them for shipping. Then all we have left are the people that are hard to buy for, and of course, a few more things for the kids.

Exchanging gifts is a long-standing Christmas tradition, especially in the West. The tradition is loosely tied to the first Christmas, when God sent his Son into the world. Jesus is God's gift to lost humanity. The Scripture calls him God's "indescribable gift" (2 Cor. 9:15), the one "in whom are hidden all the treasures of wisdom and knowledge" (Col. 2:3).

When God first gave us this marvelous gift, there were some men who rightly sensed the need to reciprocate, to respond to God with a gift of their own. These men were the Magi, the Wise Men from the east who visited Jesus at Bethlehem. "On coming to the house, they saw the child with his mother Mary, and they bowed down and worshiped him. Then they opened their treasures and presented him with gifts of gold and of incense and of myrrh" (Matt. 2:11).

The worship the Magi offered was significant because they were kings in their own right. Thus by bowing down in worship, they were acknowledging Jesus as the King of kings. Their adoration was also the fulfillment of a biblical prophecy. Concerning the coming Messiah, Isaiah had prophesied: "Nations will come to your light, and kings to the brightness of your dawn" (Isa. 60:3). That promise began to be fulfilled almost as soon as Jesus was born. The Magi represented the nations that would come to worship Christ.

The treasure they brought was also significant. The gifts were costly, and thus they demonstrated the worthiness of the One to whom they were given. But there was also something important about the gifts themselves. Gold is a gift fit for a king. It is a symbol of royalty. In the ancient world incense was often used for religious worship, as it was in the tabernacle (Ex. 30:1; 40:5; Heb. 9:4). In the Bible it also represents the prayers of the saints. David said, "May my prayer be set before you like incense" (Ps. 141:2a), and in the book of Revelation "the smoke of the incense, together with the prayers of the saints, went up before God" (Rev. 8:4). Myrrh was used in the embalming process as a spice to prepare the dead for burial.

Each of these gifts was uniquely appropriate for Christ because each was prophetic of some aspect of his saving work. Gold is for kings, and Jesus came to be the King. The Magi worshiped him as the King of the Jews, but now, by his resurrection from the dead, he is crowned as "the ruler of the kings of the earth" (Rev. 1:5). Incense is for priests, and Jesus is our High Priest, the one who offers our prayers up to God.

Jesus also offered himself as the sacrifice for our sins. In its description of his death, the Bible mentions two details specifically involving myrrh. One concerns the drink that Jesus was offered on the cross: wine mixed with myrrh (Mark 15:23). The other concerns the spices that were used to prepare his body for burial: "Nicodemus brought a mixture of myrrh and aloes, about seventy-five pounds. Taking Jesus' body, the two of them [Nicodemus and Joseph of Arimathea] wrapped it, with the spices, in strips of linen" (John 19:39–40a). These details remind us of the Magi, whose gift of myrrh hinted already back in Bethlehem that Jesus was born to die.

At the first Christmas gifts of eternal significance were exchanged. The gift of God was a Son to be our Savior. The gift of the Magi was the treasure of the nations, symbolizing the kingship of Christ and his saving death.

When it comes to Christmas gifts today, the most important thing is to receive the gift that God has given. The words on the popular Christmas card are true: "Wise Men Still Seek Him." God has sent his Son Jesus Christ to be our Savior. Everyone who believes in Jesus Christ receives the free gift of eternal life. The next thing to do is to offer ourselves back to God in worship, the way the Magi did. The treasure we offer is not gold, or frankincense, or myrrh, but our lives for his service. This is the really important gift exchange that needs to take place at Christmas.

The presents we give to one another are trivial by comparison. It is not wrong to give them, of course. But if we decide to give someone a gift, then we should do it in a way that reflects something of God's grace. A good deal of our gift giving is reciprocal: we give presents to people who will give presents to us. One is reminded of the famous words of Thomas Hobbes: "No man giveth, but with intention of good to himself."

In our family we go through an increasingly elaborate ritual that involves the drawing of names and the exchange of lists, usually complete with catalog numbers and ordering information. Almost nothing is left to chance, which of course makes it easier to get people something they actually need or want. But if we are Christians, then at least some of our giving ought to be completely gracious. We should find ways of giving to people who are truly in need, and who have no claim on our generosity. For when we were truly in need, without any claim on God's grace, he sent us the greatest gift ever.

# Part Seven

# THE BIBLE

*We believe the Bible to be the Word of God, the only infallible rule of faith and practice, and we believe the Bible must be the treasure most valued and attended to in the church's life.*

JAMES MONTGOMERY BOICE

THERE IS A FAMINE IN THE LAND. It is not a famine of bread. Farmers still have grain standing in the fields and the shelves at the bakery are full. It is not a famine of drink. The rain is falling, the reservoirs are full, and water is flowing from the tap. Nevertheless, there is a famine in the land, and because of it, the spirits of men and women are parched and dry; children are crying out for the food that will satisfy their souls. It is a famine like the one Amos prophesied, "not a famine of food or a thirst for water, but a famine of hearing the words of the LORD" (Amos 8:11).

We see the signs of this famine everywhere we look. Children are spiritually malnourished. They are not familiar with the stories of the Bible. They haven't read the Gospels or memorized any Bible verses. They do not know what God has said in his Word. By the time they get to university, they are still biblically illiterate. In the words of one college professor, the Bible remains "The Greatest Story Never Read."

As a result, the Christian worldview does not permeate our public life. With the exception of one or two cable networks, people do not mention the Bible much on television. Scripture is referred to but rarely in newspapers and magazines. Most legal, political, and social discussions take place without any reference to biblical truth.

We would like to hope that the situation is somewhat better in the church, but sometimes we have to wonder. Americans own more Bibles than any culture in the history of the world, but only one in four people under thirty read their Bibles even once a week. There is a famine in the land!

Famine is the right word to use to describe this situation because neglecting to read the Bible is life threatening. It is only by hearing God's Word that we come to faith in Jesus Christ and receive the free gift of eternal life. Jesus said it himself: "Man does not live on bread alone, but on every word that comes from the mouth of God" (Matt. 4:4).

If the Bible comes straight from God, then we need to believe it. We need to defend its historical and theological accuracy, as the following essays do. And we need to read it for our spiritual food. As James Montgomery Boice wrote in one of his *Hymns for a Modern Reformation,*

> *God's Word was written to be read,*
> *to be our life and daily bread,*
> *to guide our thoughts throughout the night*
> *and lead us forth by morning's light.*
> *So let us read, mark, learn, digest*
> *God's Word which gives us heaven's best.* [1]

# 36

# ENGLISH STANDARD VERSION

*Sola Scriptura* ("Scripture Alone") was one of the great principles of the Protestant Reformers, who wanted all Christian doctrine and the whole Christian life to rest on the solid foundation of God's Word. Over against the Roman Catholic Church, which based its theology on both Scripture and tradition, the Reformers put their trust in Scripture alone.

One of the first things that the Reformers had to do was translate the Bible into words that people could actually understand. Men like Martin Luther believed that "man shall not live by bread alone, but by every word that comes from the mouth of God" (Matt. 4:4 ESV). However, at the time of the Reformation, the Word of God was only available in Latin, the language of scholars. Although several attempts had been made to translate parts of the Bible into English—most notably by John Wycliffe—the vast majority of Christians had never read any portion of the Bible in their own language.

Even among the clergy biblical illiteracy was widespread. On one occasion the English Reformer William Tyndale got into a heated argument with a Catholic priest. He became so frustrated with the man's ignorance of the Scriptures that he cried out, "I defy the pope and all his laws, and if God spare my life, ere many years I will cause a boy that driveth the plough shall know more of the Scriptures than thou doest." Tyndale made good on his promise, translating the entire New Testament and many parts of the Old Testament into common English. This was illegal, and eventually the Catholics burned Tyndale at the stake. But by that time he had rekindled a flame that still burns today—the flame of biblical truth.

The reformation is not a thing of the past, but remains our calling in the present. One example of modern reformation is the ongoing work of Bible translation. There is a new translation that promises to help the church in its ongoing reformation. It is called the English Standard Version, or ESV. I have followed this project closely from its earliest stages because, my father—Dr. Leland Ryken of Wheaton College—served as literary stylist. (I mention this in the interest of full disclosure.)

The primary aim of the English Standard Version is to provide precise word-for-word accuracy. This immediately distinguishes it from nearly every other recent English translation. Contemporary Bible translators generally aim for what they call "dynamic" or "functional" equivalence. Instead of simply communicating what the Bible says, they try to explain what it means. For example, the phrase "God is my rock" is translated "God is my firm support." God is a firm support, of course, and that may be part of what the Bible means, but the problem is that the English reader no longer knows what the Bible *says*. Or consider another example: In Ephesians 5:2 the New International Version (NIV) exhorts us to "live a life of love." However, what the Scripture actually says is "Walk in love," which, among other things, reminds us that the Christian life is a pilgrimage.

The advantage of a word-for-word translation is that it keeps us close to the original biblical text. This is especially important when it comes to understanding some of the classic theological vocabulary of Scripture. The ESV restores the important term "propitiation" (which was removed from the NIV) to the biblical text. Thus Romans 3 reads: "For all have sinned and fall short of the glory of God, and are justified by his grace as a gift, through the redemption that is in Christ Jesus, whom God put forward as a propitiation by his blood, to be received by faith" (Rom.

3:23–25). This is one example of the way a more literal translation can help promote sound theology.

The English Standard Version is also superior from the literary standpoint. This is partly because it inherits the rich cadences of the King James Version. The ESV stands in the classic stream of literal Bible translations that began during the Protestant Reformation. This tradition runs from William Tyndale's New Testament in 1526, through the King James Version (KJV) in 1611, to the American Standard Version (ASV) of 1901 and the Revised Standard Version (RSV) of 1952 and 1971. The King James Version has always been the best translation for public reading because the scholars who produced it had an ear for spoken English, and thus carefully alternated between stressed and unstressed syllables. The English Standard Version largely retains the dignity and beauty of the King James Version.

At the same time, the ESV is partly based on the Revised Standard Version, or RSV. The RSV is an excellent translation. Among other things, it updates some of the old-fashioned language of the KJV. However, evangelicals have always rejected the RSV, mainly because the liberal scholars who produced it mistranslated some key biblical texts. But when the editors at the evangelical publishing house Crossway Books were given the opportunity to revise the RSV, they jumped at the chance. For several years a team of evangelical scholars carefully scrutinized every word in the Bible to produce a literal and literary translation for all of life.

I use the English Standard Version both for my own personal Bible reading and for my pulpit ministry. I believe it is the translation I have been waiting for all my life, but get a copy and make your own evaluation. Or at least read a copy of any decent English translation. The reformation of the church always begins with reading the Bible. If you study the Bible every day, then you are making a personal commitment to *sola Scriptura*. Indeed, in your own quiet way, you are working for a modern reformation.

# 37

# THE NEW NIV

In 2002 the International Bible Society produced a revision of the New International Version, commonly known as the NIV. The distinctive feature of the new translation was its use of gender-neutral language. Although the Bible was only published in Britain, there were also plans to release it here in America. However, under a storm of protest from conservative critics, the International Bible Society was forced to change its plans.

At the time, the Society published a statement that it had "abandoned all plans for gender-related changes in future editions of the New International Version." That explains why the release of Today's New International Version, or TNIV, came as a shock. The Society seems to have gone back on its promise. As its name suggests, and as its editors admit, the TNIV is in fact a revision of the NIV.

Conservative Christians have been quick to attack the TNIV, partly out of a sense of betrayal. "Today's New International Perversion," screamed one headline. Unfortunately, as is typically the case, many people have made up their minds about the TNIV without actually studying it. The question is, How accurate is the new translation? While in some respects the TNIV is an improvement, some of its changes make it less than fully reliable for the church.

Curiously, although the main justification for the TNIV is its supposed "gender accuracy," the "Word to the Reader" at the front of the

Bible says little about this. It speaks vaguely about how "diverse and complex cultural forces continue to bring about subtle shifts in the meanings and/or connotations of even old, well-established words and phrases." But the main thing that supporters of the TNIV talk about is its gender usage.

Here it must be said that in some cases, the TNIV *is* an improvement. One good example is Romans 3:28. The NIV says, "For we maintain that a man is justified by faith apart from observing the law" (Rom. 3:28). Obviously, justification is not for men only, but for everyone who believes. So the TNIV is not wrong to say "a *person* is justified by faith" (Rom. 3:28; cf. Gal. 2:16).

There are some problems with the TNIV, however. In an effort to get rid of words like "man" and "men," "him" and "he," the TNIV often changes masculine, third person, singular pronouns into plural, gender-neutral pronouns. For example, whereas in the NIV Jesus says "If anyone hears my voice and opens the door, I will come in and eat with him, and he with me" (Rev. 3:20), the TNIV has this: "If anyone hears my voice and opens the door, I will come in and eat with them, and they with me" (Rev. 3:20). This distorts the Bible's emphasis on personal responsibility, or on God's relationship with the individual Christian (see also John 6:50; Heb. 9:27).

As a general rule, the TNIV also replaces the words "son" and "sons" with "children" or "people." This is also a distortion, because it removes the biblical emphasis on the rights of sonship, which in biblical times included inheritance (e.g. Gal. 4:5). At times the word "brother" is replaced with words like "someone" or "person," and the word "father" is changed to "parent." For example, the TNIV translates Hebrews 12:7 like this: "Endure hardship as discipline; God is treating you as his children [not "sons"]. For what children are not disciplined by their parents [rather than "father"]?" (Heb. 12:7). By eliminating the original metaphor, this translation alters the meaning of the biblical text.

Such changes unnecessarily accommodate biblical language to contemporary culture. There are many places where the Bible intends to use language in a gender-specific way, and in these places its intention should not be thwarted. Perhaps the most unfortunate example is Hebrews 2:6, where the TNIV asks, "What are mere mortals that you are mindful of them, human beings that you care for them?" People who are familiar with this verse will recognize that the theologically significant phrase "son of man" has disappeared. But what about people who *don't* know the verse?

Other changes are not gender-related, but deserve to be mentioned. The word "saints" has been replaced with phrases like "God's people" (Rom. 8:27), which is true enough, but loses the original emphasis on holiness, and also the connection with sanctification. If the word needed to be replaced—which is debatable—it might have been better to use "holy ones" as a substitute.

The TNIV sometimes changes the word "Jews" to "Jewish leaders" (e.g. John 19:12; Acts 13:50). This change is motivated by concerns about anti-Semitism, but again this is unnecessary. Matthew and John were hardly anti-Semites! They said "Jews" rather than "Jewish leaders" because they wanted to show the corporate responsibility of their own people for the Messiah's death, just as they wanted to show that their people could find salvation through his resurrection.

Much of the recent outcry over the TNIV has been all too hysterical. However, it must also be said that by suddenly going back on its former agreement, the International Bible Society has done its part to arouse the opposition. In the long run, the important question is whether the new version is suitable for Christians who believe in the inerrancy of Scripture. While recognizing that no translation is perfect, I cannot give the TNIV my unqualified support. In fact, I have signed a public statement that says, "In light of troubling translation inaccuracies—primarily (but not exclusively) in relation to gender language—that introduce distortion to the meanings that were conveyed better by the original NIV, we cannot endorse the TNIV translation as sufficiently accurate to commend to the church."

I am especially concerned that people who use and trust the NIV will become confused. The TNIV is *not* the NIV, and has introduced some unfortunate changes. And as for the verses where the TNIV is an improvement, many of the same improvements are already available in the English Standard Version (ESV). This is because the translators of the ESV were concerned to use gender-neutral language, with one important qualification: they would only do so where this could be done without losing significant aspects of the original meaning.[1]

## 38

# THE PRAYER OF JABEZ

Who ever would have thought that Jabez would become a bestseller? For thousands of years the poor man has been languishing in obscurity, stuck between Hazzobebah and Kelub in an Old Testament genealogy. But a book about this obscure biblical figure made the *New York Times* list for Advice, How-to & Miscellaneous books.

The book was written by Bruce Wilkinson, an evangelical preacher well known for his Walk Thru the Bible seminars. Wilkinson has been using the prayer of Jabez for thirty years, ever since he first learned it from a seminary chaplain. The prayer is based on the following verses: "Jabez was more honorable than his brothers. His mother had named him Jabez, saying, 'I gave birth to him in pain.' Jabez cried out to the God of Israel, 'Oh, that you would bless me and enlarge my territory! Let your hand be with me, and keep me from harm so that I will be free from pain.' And God granted his request" (1 Chron. 4:9–10).

Although this is the only place Jabez is mentioned in the entire Bible, the man's prayer has taken Christendom by storm. Well over three million copies of his book have been sold. Web sites list personal testimonies of unusual answers to his prayer. A video series is in the works, as are special versions of the book for children, teens, and women. Churches host Jabez study groups and Jabez seminars. I received a request to host one at Tenth Presbyterian Church in place of our usual Sunday morning service. The promotional literature said, "If the principles of this message are taken seriously, this event could produce a major turning point in the spiritual growth and priorities of your congregation, and perhaps spark a revival in your community." Perhaps. But it is worth asking whether the prayer of Jabez is, as its author claims, "the key to a life of extraordinary favor with God."

It should be emphasized that all the prayers in the Bible—including the one that Jabez prayed—help set the agenda for our intercession. One of the best ways to learn how to pray is to pray through the Scriptures. The rediscovery of an Old Testament prayer is especially welcome—and from Chronicles, of all places.

It should also be said that some of Wilkinson's teaching is helpful. For example, he emphasizes that the prayer is for spiritual rather than material blessings. Even the petition "enlarge my territory" is interpreted as a request for the biggest possible field for evangelism. It is doubtful whether that is what Jabez had in mind, but at least Wilkinson tries to discourage people from praying primarily for financial prosperity.

At the same time, however, he does encourage Christians to pray more selfishly. "Is it possible," he asks, "that God wants you to be more 'selfish' in your prayers?" This self-centered focus seems to be the key to "praying Jabez." In the words of one bookseller, "Everybody is looking to expand their territory." Indeed, it is hard to think of a prayer more likely to appeal to Americans than one that petitions for territorial expansion.

There are a number of theological problems with Wilkinson's book. One is its insistence on asking for miracles. People who use the prayer of Jabez are promised "a front-row seat in a life of miracles." "It's when you thrust yourself in the mainstream of God's plans for this world . . . that you release miracles."[1] Wilkinson's view of God's sovereignty is also problematic. He argues that Christians who do not "pray Jabez" will miss out on the blessings God has in store for them. "If you didn't ask Him for a blessing yesterday," Wilkinson writes, "you didn't get all you were supposed to have."[2] By this reasoning, a believer who forgets to pray Jabez is relegated to Plan B of divine providence.

There is also the danger of turning Jabez into a mantra rather than offering it as a genuine prayer. Putting faith in the words of a particular prayer tends to turn that prayer into a work. In the words of one secular observer, "It's very evangelical and very American, this whole notion that if you know the right technique, the right form, that prayer will be efficient and effective." That is exactly what *The Prayer of Jabez* offers: a simple technique that guarantees spiritual blessing. So we are assured that "thousands of believers who are applying [the prayer's] truths are seeing miracles happen on a regular basis."[3]

Perhaps the biggest problem is the Jabez mindset. Every few years another fad invades the evangelical church. It is always presented as the secret to a life of happiness, blessing, sanctification, and so on. The word for this way of thinking is *gnosticism*. The Gnostic claims to have secret knowledge that goes beyond ordinary religious experience. Anyone who gains this knowledge breaks through to a whole new level of spiritual experience.

If Jabez really is the key to a better prayer life, one wonders where that leaves the Lord's Prayer. When the disciples asked Jesus how to pray, he did not say, "How to pray!? You're kidding, right? Haven't I ever told you guys about Jabez?" Instead, he gave his disciples a new model for prayer. Unlike the prayer of Jabez, the prayer of Jesus is not a selfish prayer. It is not even offered in the first person. All of its petitions are corporate: give *us,* forgive *us,* deliver *us.* Nor did Jesus teach us to pray for miracles. Instead, he taught us to do simple, ordinary things like worship God's holy name, ask for what we need, confess our sins, and seek God's heavenly kingdom and sovereign will.

# 39

# THE BOX FOR HIS BROTHER'S BONES

In the summer of 2002, an anonymous collector asked the French paleographer Andre Lemaire to examine the inscription on an ancient ossuary from Jerusalem. An ossuary is a box for burying people's bones. This particular ossuary—which was empty apart from a few bone fragments—was made of limestone and measured twenty inches long, ten inches wide, and twelve inches high. For just a few hundred dollars, the collector had bought it more than a decade ago from someone who claimed that it was found just south of the Mount of Olives, in an area dotted with burial caves.

The inscription excited Lemaire as soon as he read it, and since its public announcement, it has excited people all over the world. Its words are simple. They read: "James, son of Joseph, brother of Jesus."

The obvious question is whether the inscription refers to Jesus of Nazareth, also called the Christ. If so, then the James in question was one of the great men of the early church—not the apostle, but the brother of Jesus, the leader of the Christian community in Jerusalem, and the man who wrote the well-known epistle of James.

The first step was to determine whether the inscription actually dated to the first century. It probably does, although some scholars refute this finding. For one thing, it is written in the style of Aramaic script common to that period. Furthermore, there is a patina on the ossuary—the dust of time. Experts from the Geological Institute of Israel who have examined it agree that it dates to around A.D. 60. They believe that the inscription is not a fake. It also fits what we know about James, who was martyred in A.D. 62. In the words of Josephus, the ancient historian, the high priest Ananus killed "one James, the brother of Jesus who was called Christ."

The next step is to consider whether the names James, Joseph, and Jesus could refer to anyone else. All three names were relatively common in the first century—like Tom, Dick, and Harry—so it is not surprising to find them on an ossuary from that period. However, the odds are strongly against there being another family with the same three names in the same order. But the clincher is that James's brother is mentioned at all. Ordinarily such an inscription would refer only to the deceased, and possibly to his father. It is exceptionally rare to mention his brother at all. The only reason for doing so would be if his brother happened to be famous. This confirms beyond reasonable doubt that the ossuary was for James, the brother of Jesus Christ.

This discovery has stirred up a certain amount of theological controversy. According to the official Roman Catholic interpretation, Jesus did not have any brothers—at least not any full brothers. In order to defend their belief that Mary was a perpetual virgin, Catholics argue that Mary and Joseph never had intercourse and thus never had any more children. The brothers of Jesus mentioned in the New Testament must have been Joseph's sons by a previous marriage, or perhaps they were Jesus' cousins (this is the traditional Eastern Orthodox view).

The ossuary creates problems for the Catholic view because it helps confirm that James and Jesus were brothers. But there never was any biblical evidence for the Catholic position. It was based entirely on beliefs about Mary that come from tradition and not from Scripture. Protestants have always believed that Mary and Joseph did have more children and that James was one of their sons. We believe this because the Bible clearly identifies James as one of Jesus' brothers (Matt. 13:55).

His identity as the brother of our Lord explains why James rose to such a prominent position in the early church. Although he never gets the attention that Peter and Paul receive, James played a major role in shaping the New Testament church. At the famous Jerusalem Council in Acts 15, it was James who had the last word. In those days this privilege was reserved for the man with the most authority. And it was James—not Peter or Paul—who commanded the greatest respect. This was because, in Jewish culture, when the oldest son died the mantle of responsibility fell on the shoulders of his next oldest brother. So after Jesus returned to heaven, it was only natural for people to look to his brother James as one of their leaders.

The James ossuary is already being hailed as the most important archaeological discovery since the Dead Sea Scrolls—the first great find of the twenty-first century. If scholars are right, then its inscription is the earliest extra-biblical mention of Jesus Christ.

What difference does the ossuary make? Does it prove anything about Jesus? The box for his brother's bones provides tangible evidence that Jesus was a real person with a real family. But any reasonable historian will tell you that the New Testament proved this already. The real question is not whether Jesus ever lived, but whether he is anything more than just a man. And on this point hardened skeptics will remain unconvinced. It will take more than reading the name "Jesus" on an old box of bones to make them believe that Jesus Christ is the Son of God and the Savior of sinners. These are things that people can only accept by faith.

This was as true for James as it is for anyone else. At first James was a skeptic. Like the rest of Jesus' brothers, he didn't understand who Jesus was or what he had come to do. As we read in the gospels, "even his own brothers did not believe in him" (John 7:5).

But eventually Jesus proved himself to James. He appeared to him after he rose from the dead (1 Cor. 15:7). James responded by faith, and from that point on he identified himself, not simply as the brother of Jesus, but as "a servant of the Lord Jesus Christ" (James 1:1). James began to worship Jesus as his Savior and Lord. And this means that one day his old bones will come back to life, because everyone who believes in Jesus will be raised to eternal glory.[1]

# Part Eight

# CHURCH
# HISTORY

*Church history makes the gospel intelligible by keeping ever
before us the reality that the divine work of salvation takes places in
and even depends upon things human. This does not mean that humans
or the material of creation cooperate with God in the work of
redemption. It simply means that without the human form and the rest
of created matter there is no salvation or gospel as we know it. . . .
[T]hings human are not really a problem but in fact provide the arena
that allows God to reveal himself in his most glorious proportions.*

D. G. HART

I HAVE AN ONGOING INTEREST in church his-
tory. This is partly because the history of Christianity has been an area
of special study and interest for me. It is also because I know its value
for the contemporary church. Looking to the past helps us know how
to live for God in the present and the future.

Studying church history helps us do this in several different ways.
The history of doctrine helps us understand why we believe what we
believe, as well as what we have chosen not to believe. It teaches us to
discern between what is true and what is false in theology. Church his-

tory also helps us know how to behave. The story of God's people through time includes many inspiring examples of heroic courage and enduring faith. Then there is the other side of church history: a sordid tale of failure and depravity. But even this is edifying, because it shows that whatever we accomplish for God is done in spite of ourselves, by the working of his grace.

However, church history has a deeper significance than the practical lessons we can draw from it. One of the theologians who understood this best was Jonathan Edwards, the famous preacher of the Great Awakening. Edwards believed that the center of history is the saving love of God in Jesus Christ, and that this alone gives the history of the church— and indeed the history of the world—its true significance. In his landmark biography, historian George Marsden offers the following summary of Edwards' Christ-centered approach to history: "The history of redemption was the very purpose of creation. Nothing in human history had significance on its own, any more than created nature had significance on its own. Christ's saving love was the center of all history and defined its meaning."[1]

Church history testifies to the saving grace of Jesus Christ. Or to put it another way, one of the ways God speaks to us is through the history of his people in the world. The chapters that follow touch briefly on five important episodes in church history. In addition to showing us what to believe and how to behave, they bear witness to God's redeeming love for us in Jesus Christ.

# THE CHURCH MOTHERS

Everyone knows about the Church Fathers. They were men like Jerome, Athanasius, and Augustine. These were the great theologians who helped organize the church's thinking on central Christian doctrines such as the Trinity and the Incarnation. But what about the Church Mothers? Why doesn't anyone ever talk about them? The truth is that there were some great women in the early church, and that they too have left us their legacy.

A striking testimony to the character of Christian women in those days comes from the famous preacher John Chrysostom, whose father died while he was an infant, and who thus was raised by his mother Anthousa. Through the years this godly widow made many sacrifices to educate her children. Eventually Chrysostom was able to study with Libanios, the famous rhetoric teacher at Antioch. When Libanios learned of the costly and courageous way Anthousa had raised her family, he looked around at his pupils and said: "Great heavens, what remarkable women are to be found among the Christians!"[1]

There were many women like Anthousa in the early church. They were not great theologians, if by that we mean someone whose thinking and writing helped to shape Christian theology for generations to come. But many of the Church Mothers were good theologians who carefully studied the Scriptures so they could live for the glory of God.

One of these women was the Roman widow Marcella. Marcella was a friend of the great Bible scholar Jerome, who praised her passion to know what the Bible really said. She was like the Bereans whom the apostle Paul commended for "examin[ing] the Scriptures every day" to make sure that what he said was true (Acts 17:11). According to Jerome,

> [Marcella] never came without asking something about Scripture, nor did she immediately accept my explanation as satisfactory, but she proposed questions from the opposite viewpoint, not for the sake of being contentious, but so that by asking, she might learn. . . . What virtue I found in her, what cleverness, what holiness, what purity. . . . I will say only this, that whatever in us was gathered by long study and by lengthy meditation . . . this she tasted, this she learned, this she possessed. Thus after my departure, if an argument arose about some evidence from Scripture, the question was pursued with her as the judge.[2]

Another of Jerome's close female friends was a wealthy woman named Paula. Paula did many good things for the sake of the gospel. But in a letter written shortly after her death, Jerome especially praised her intellect, and her thirst for biblical knowledge: "She had memorized the Scripture. . . . [S]he urged me that she, along with her daughter, might read through the Old and New Testaments. . . . If at any passage I was at a loss and frankly confessed that I was ignorant, she by no means wanted to rest content with my reply, but by fresh questions would force me to say which of the many possible meanings seemed to me the most likely."[3]

Some of the Church Mothers were, in fact, mothers. Probably the most famous was Augustine's mother, Monica. The great joy of Monica's life was to see both her pagan husband and her rebellious son receive Jesus Christ as Savior and Lord. Although she had catechized Augustine in his youth, for many years he turned his back on the Christian faith. But Monica did not despair. She kept praying for her son's salvation, and eventually Augustine came back to Christ. Monica's motherly intercession was the great work of her life, and the legacy that her son left the church was also her legacy.

Not all the Church Mothers had children of their own. Some of them were single. One of the significant women in John Chrysostom's life was Olympias, the famous deaconess of Constantinople. Olympias had a personal fortune that she willingly dedicated to the needs of the poor. She also took an active role in church life. In the words of one ancient historian, "She contended eagerly in no minor contests for the name of the truth, taught many women, held solemn conversations with priests, honored the bishops, and was deemed worthy to be a confessor on behalf of truth."[4] Everything she did was adorned with personal godliness. An ancient biographical work entitled *The Life of Olympias, Deaconess* describes her as having "an appearance without pretense, character without affectation . . . a mind without vainglory, intelligence without conceit . . . character without limits, immeasurable self-control . . . the ornament of all the humble."[5]

These are only a few of the Church Mothers mentioned by the Church Fathers. There are others, such as Melania, Proba, and Macrina, the sister of two famous theologians: Gregory of Nyssa and Basil the Great. And of course, there were many other women whose names have been forgotten. They studied the Bible, prayed for their children, and cared for the sick and the poor. The Church Mothers set a high standard for all the Christian women—and all the Christian men—who follow.

The way to claim the inheritance these women left behind is to live in close communion with Christ, being devoted to his teaching. Be like Mary, who sat at Jesus' feet to learn theology, and of whom it was said: "Mary has chosen what is better, and it will not be taken away from her" (Luke 10:42b). If you have children, teach them to follow Christ and pray for their salvation. Be like Eunice, whose faith came to life in the ministry of her son Timothy (2 Tim. 1:5). And remain active in service and mercy. Be like Dorcas, "who was always doing good and helping the poor" (Acts 9:36). The church needs mothers like these in every generation.[6]

# 41

# DIET OF WORMS

It is customary to date the beginning of the Protestant Reformation to October 31, 1517, the day on which a young German monk and Bible scholar named Martin Luther nailed his famous "Ninety-five Theses" to the door of the Wittenburg church.

Luther's document attacked the common Roman Catholic practice of allowing people to reduce the punishment for their sins by buying indulgences. His "Ninety-five Theses" also gave the first inklings of his major personal and theological breakthrough: the doctrine of justification by faith alone.

Luther needed a breakthrough because he had long been troubled by his sins. How could an unrighteous man like himself serve a righteous God? As he later wrote: "Though I lived as a monk without reproach, I felt that I was a sinner before God with an extremely disturbed conscience. I could not believe that he was placated by my satisfaction. I did not love, yes, I hated the righteous God who punishes sinners, and secretly, if not blasphemously, certainly murmuring greatly, I was angry with God."[1]

What especially troubled Luther was Paul's announcement at the beginning of his epistle to the Romans: "In the gospel a righteousness from God is revealed, a righteousness that is by faith from first to last" (Rom.

1:17). This verse was a terror to Luther because the only righteousness he had ever heard of was the kind that destroyed sinners like himself.

Then Luther had his breakthrough:

> At last, by the mercy of God, meditating day and night, I gave heed to the context of the words, namely, "In it the righteousness of God is revealed, as it is written, 'He who through faith is righteous shall live.' " There I began to understand that the righteousness of God is that by which the righteous lives by a gift of God, namely by faith. And this is the meaning: the righteousness of God is revealed by the gospel, namely, the passive righteousness with which merciful God justifies us by faith, as it is written, "He who's faith is righteous shall live." Here I felt that I was altogether born again and had entered paradise itself through open gates.[2]

That was the beginning of the Reformation, but only the beginning. Luther soon attracted the attention of the pope, not so much for his doctrine of justification as for his criticism of the church. But during the next several years it would still have been possible for the church to have been reformed without being divided. It was not until the Diet of Worms that the break between the Reformers and the Catholics became final, which is why that meeting, which took place in April of 1521, was the most significant event in the church history of the sixteenth century.

Luther had been summoned to Worms by the Holy Roman Emperor himself, Charles V. When the Reformer entered the imperial chamber, he found his writings spread out on the table. These were the writings the emperor wanted Luther to recant, declaring publicly that everything he had ever written about the gospel and the church was mistaken.

Luther hardly knew what to say. Some of his works were devotional writings which no one would wish to recant. Others contained criticisms of the Roman Catholic church which no one could deny. Yet Luther was aware that some of his other writings contained harsh criticisms he perhaps ought to recant. But this he would only do on one condition, namely, that someone expose his errors "by the writings of the prophets and the evangelists." "Once I have been taught," Luther went on to say, "I shall be quite ready to renounce every error, and I shall be the first to cast my books into the fire."

This was hardly the answer the emperor and his counselors were looking for, especially since they did not have the theological expertise to refute Luther themselves. Again they pressed him to repudiate his doctrine. Finally, Luther spoke his famous words:

> Unless I am convinced by the testimony of the Scriptures or by clear reason (for I do not trust either in the pope or in councils alone, since it is well known that they have often erred and contradicted themselves), I am bound by the Scriptures I have quoted and my conscience is captive to the Word of God. I cannot and I will not retract anything, since it is neither safe nor right to go against conscience. God help me. Amen. Here I stand, I cannot do otherwise.[3]

With these words, Luther staked all his theological claims on the second great principle of the Reformation: Scripture alone. For the churches of the Reformation, the Bible and the Bible alone was the final authority for Christian faith and practice.

When Luther refused to place the authority of the church on a par with the authority of Scripture, he was taking a stand that would end up dividing the church. And rightly so! The church can only be the church when it preaches the gospel of salvation by grace alone through faith alone in Christ alone, as it is taught in Scripture alone.

The great doctrines of the Reformation are as badly needed today as they were in the sixteenth century. Pope John Paul II announced that he would grant an indulgence to anyone who made a pilgrimage to Israel during the year 2000. This is just one example of the way the Roman Catholic Church still encourages its members to pay for their sins by doing good works. For this and many other reasons, the world still needs to hear the voice of Martin Luther, who wrote the following paraphrase of Psalm 130:[4]

From trouble deep I cry to thee,
Lord God, hear thou my crying;
Thy gracious ear, oh, turn to me,
Open it to my sighing.
For if thou mean'st to look upon
The wrong and evil that is done,
Who, Lord, can stand before thee?
With thee counts nothing but thy grace
To cover all our failing.
The best life cannot win the race,
Good works are unavailing.
Before thee no one glory can,
And so must tremble every man,
And live by thy grace only.[5]

# 42

# THE WESTMINSTER ASSEMBLY

Of all the things that happened during the seventeenth century, the most important for Presbyterians was the Westminster Assembly, which met from 1643 to 1649. During those years, the Westminster Divines—so called because they were experts in "divinity," which meant "theology"—prepared the theological documents that form the basis for Presbyterian theology and practice to this day.

Unfortunately, many Presbyterians are relatively unfamiliar with the Westminster Standards and the history behind them. That history contains a number of surprises. For one thing, the Westminster Assembly met during a time of war. Those were the days of the English Civil War, when Parliament was fighting against Charles I. As battles were won and lost all over Britain, the Westminster Divines patiently went about their work from one year to the next.

Here is another surprise: The Assembly met at the request of Parliament. The Puritans in England and the Presbyterians in Scotland had joined forces against the Crown, especially because Charles I had tried to impose many Roman Catholic practices on the Anglican church. The

Scottish Presbyterians and the English Puritans were allies; however, there were some theological differences between them, so Parliament asked the best theological minds in Britain to agree on a doctrinal statement for both countries. In the end, more than one hundred English pastors and theologians, aided by thirty members of Parliament (both lords and commoners) and a crack team of six scholars from Scotland, were named to the Assembly. Around seventy of them were able to participate on any given day, and they met at Westminster Abbey in London; hence the name: Westminster Assembly.

The progress of the Assembly was slow, largely because their rules allowed for unlimited debate. Yet the Westminster Divines eventually produced five major documents:

- a Form of Government to help organize the church in the Presbyterian way, which means "decently and in order" (1 Cor. 14:40 NKJV), under the spiritual authority of elders;
- a Directory of Worship to help praise God in the biblical way, conducting services "according to the Word of God"—by his design rather than man's desire;
- a Confession of Faith to explain biblical doctrine in a systematic way; and
- two catechisms for teaching theology through questions and answers: the Shorter Catechism for those who were "common and unlearned," and the Larger Catechism for those "of understanding."

One interesting note about the Shorter Catechism: The Westminster Divines first produced the Larger Catechism, but Parliament sent it back and asked the Assembly for something easier to understand.

The Westminster Standards contain the essential *biblical* truths about God and man that all Christians everywhere have always professed: that there is only one God, who exists in three persons, who made everything there is, and who saves us by his grace. It is *Reformed* theology; that is to say, it is the theology of the Protestant Reformation. The Westminster Confession of Faith was written after the church had an entire century to spend learning and perfecting the doctrine taught by Martin Luther, John Calvin, and the other Reformers. Reformation theology, which is based on the Bible alone, teaches that salvation comes by grace alone, through faith alone, in Christ alone, to the glory of God alone. The Westminster Standards are also *covenantal* in their theology. They are centered on God's covenant of grace with his people. Finally, they are *evangelical* in their theology. They proclaim the good news of salvation from sin through the death and resurrection of Jesus Christ.

There is one final surprise about the Westminster Standards: Despite the fact that they were written in London, they never held very much influence in England. Eventually the monarchy came back into power, the Puritans were defeated and persecuted, and the church reverted to Anglicanism. Yet the work of the Westminster Divines has long remained the standard for Presbyterians and also many Baptists in Scotland, America, and Korea. Therefore, it is sad to see them gradually fall into disuse in our culture. Children no longer learn their catechism and adults no longer know their confession, which is a tragic loss.

A story that illustrates the practical value of knowing Presbyterian doctrine comes from B. B. Warfield (1851–1921), the great Princeton theologian. It concerns a Christian man who traveled West during the days of the pioneers. One day he found himself in the middle of a gunfight in a wild western town. The whole town was in an uproar, but he saw one man who—despite all the commotion—remained calm, cool, and collected. The traveler was so amazed at the man's composure that he said to himself, "Now there is a man who knows his theology." At this he walked up to him and asked the first question in the Shorter Catechism, "What is the chief end of man?" The man answered correctly, "Man's chief end is to glorify God and to enjoy Him forever." On the basis of Warfield's story, I commend to you the Westminster Catechisms and Confession of Faith as a theology suitable for every situation in life.[1]

# THE GREAT AWAKENING

The eighteenth century was marked by an unusual outpouring of God's Spirit. The Great Awakening, as it is usually called, may have begun among a group of German Protestants known as the Moravians. In 1727 a nobleman named Count Zinzendorf (1700–1760) offered his property as a refuge for Christians who were persecuted for their faith. The refugees who gathered on his lands promised that they would live together in true Christian brotherhood.

Not many months after they started their community, the Moravian Brethren became conscious of a special nearness of God's presence. Their meetings were marked by passionate praise for Christ and public confession of sin. Then came the day which Zinzendorf described as "a day of the outpourings of the Holy Spirit upon the congregation." As a result of this spiritual awakening, the Moravians committed themselves to pray for the worldwide spread of the Gospel. They met in pairs to pray hour by hour around the clock, an "Hourly Intercession" which continued for more than one hundred years.

The Moravians sent missionaries to other countries, and it was at a Moravian meeting in London that the English preacher John Wesley (1703–1791) was converted. Wesley had long been a churchman, and even a missionary, but he was not a born-again Christian. "I went to

America to convert the Indians," he lamented, "but O who will convert me!" The answer turned out to be the Moravians. In 1738 Wesley attended one of their prayer meetings at Aldersgate in London. It was there that "I felt my heart strangely warmed," he later wrote. "I felt I did trust in Christ, Christ alone for salvation; and an assurance was given to me that he had taken away my sins."

Wesley became a successful evangelist throughout Britain and America, often preaching out of doors. But he was not the only one. At the same time, God was pouring out his Spirit on many ministers and many churches in many places. In Philadelphia the great Calvinist George Whitefield (1714–1770) preached the gospel to an audience estimated in the tens of thousands. In Virginia, by the providence of God, a slaveholder found a few pages torn from Thomas Boston's wonderful book *The Fourfold State of Man.* Not only was the man converted, but a revival broke out among his slaves. In Massachusetts there was revival in the church pastored by Jonathan Edwards (1703–1758). It was Edwards's grandfather Solomon Stoddard (1643–1729) who offered one of the best definitions of spiritual awakening: "There are some special Seasons wherein God doth in a remarkable Manner revive Religion among his People. God doth not always carry on his work in the church in the same Proportion . . . there be times wherein there is a plentiful Effusion of the Spirit of God, and Religion is in a more flourishing Condition."

Wherever true religion flourishes, society is transformed. Wesley, Whitefield, and Edwards preached in times that were just as immoral as our own. Substance abuse was common, chiefly in the form of alcoholism. Biblical Christians were distressed by the prevalence of sins like gambling, adultery, slavery, and infanticide. Edwards complained that "there is very little appearance of zeal for the mysterious and spiritual doctrines of Christianity; and they never were so ridiculed, and had in contempt, as they are in the present age. . . . never [was there] any age wherein was so much scoffing at, and ridiculing the gospel of Christ . . . as there is at this day."[1] Yet the Great Awakening brought significant changes. In England it probably prevented the violent kind of revolution suffered in France. In America it ensured that the United States would become a profoundly Christian nation. It led to the founding of many Ivy League institutions as explicitly Christian colleges. Most important of all, many souls were saved.

Whenever I study the Great Awakening, I feel pangs of longing. Our culture is dying a long, slow spiritual death. We would rather be entertained than edified, which is why we prefer to celebrate perversion than to forbid it, and why we prefer to take innocent life than to preserve it. The only thing that can save us is a new awakening in which "the Spirit is poured upon us from on high" (Isa. 32:15).

If God did send his Spirit to awaken us, he would come first to the church. God is always at work among us, but I sometimes wonder what the Holy Spirit would do if he visited us with a revival of biblical proportions. Probably, he would do what he did when he awakened the little church pastored by Jonathan Parsons (1705–1776) at the beginning of the Great Awakening. Here is what happened, in Parsons's own words:

> The Summer following my Ordination there was a great Effusion of the Holy Spirit upon the People. There appear'd to be an uncommon Attention to the Preaching of the Word, and . . . a remarkable Concern about Salvation. 'Twas a general Inquiry among the Middle aged and Youth, What must I do to be saved? Great Numbers came to my Study . . . under manifest Concern about their Souls. I seldom went into a House among my Neighbours, but they had some free Discourse about Religion, or were searching after the Meaning of some Texts of Scripture. . . . [I]n less than ten Months fifty-two Persons were added to the Church. There were several whole Families baptiz'd. Many of the young People were greatly reformed.[2]

That is more than we deserve, I know, but I long to see it, and it is not too much to pray for.

## 44

# THE AMERICAN CENTURY

The twentieth century was a remarkable century. The global population exploded. There are more people alive today—some six billion in all—than in the rest of history combined. There were amazing scientific discoveries, like the theory of relativity and the splitting of the atom. There were rapid technological advances: televisions, computers, and lasers; automobiles, airplanes, and space shuttles. The twentieth century will always be known as the century when we put a man on the moon.

Sadly, however, a great deal of our most creative energy went into developing new ways to kill one another: tanks, aircraft carriers, laser-guided missiles, chemical and biological weapons, and of course, the atomic bomb. For the first time in history we developed the capacity to destroy ourselves. The reason we needed all these weapons is because we spent most of the twentieth century at war. Hence the title of a book on the twentieth century—*Reflections on a Ravaged Century*.[1] First we had "the war to end all wars." Then we had another one, and afterwards we kept on fighting. Despite all our efforts to achieve worldwide peace—the United Nations, for example—there was always an armed conflict somewhere on planet earth, as if to prove that we are our own worst enemies.

It was a remarkable century, and America has been near the center of it all, which is why some observers call it "The American Century." The United States is the greatest superpower in the history of the world. Many of the century's discoveries were made on American soil, and it is, after all, an American flag that is planted on the moon. In the providence of God, we were on the winning side in both of the century's two great wars (or all three, if the "Cold War" counts). For better and for worse, our language is the world's language, our products are the world's products, and our culture is the world's culture.

What has been God's purpose in all of this? Only eternity will tell, but it seems that part of his purpose has been to prove that we cannot live without him. In a world without God we are doomed to suffer man's inhumanity to man. Think of Joseph Stalin, Adolf Hitler, and Mao Tse-Tung, not to mention all of their despicable comrades and cruel followers. Then contemplate the words of the apostle Paul: "The wrath of God is being revealed from heaven against all the godlessness and wickedness of men who suppress the truth by their wickedness. . . . Although they claimed to be wise, they became fools. . . . Therefore God . . . gave them over to a depraved mind, to do what ought not to be done. They have become filled with every kind of wickedness, evil, greed and depravity. They are full of envy, murder, strife, deceit and malice" (Rom. 1:18, 22, 28–29). Since the days of Noah, has there ever been a century which so clearly demonstrates the wrath of God against the wickedness of humanity?

In the face of all this evil, God has allowed his people to suffer. According to some estimates, there have been more martyrs in the twentieth century than in all previous centuries combined. Our own brothers and sisters languished in the gulags, were slaughtered by death squads, or were left to die in communist prisons. This, too, has been part of God's purpose. We know this because the Bible promises that we will "suffer grief in all kinds of trials . . . so that your faith . . . may be proved genuine and may result in praise, glory and honor when Jesus Christ is revealed" (1 Peter 1:6–7). Our sufferings have indeed proved that our faith is genuine. Perhaps that is why, in some of the places where the church has faced the fiercest opposition—like China and Russia—it has also witnessed the most rapid growth.

The church grew. There are more Christians alive now than in the rest of history combined. Furthermore, according to some experts, the percentage of Christians in the world population (about 34%) is as high now as it has ever been. One reason for this is that the twentieth century was a great century for missions. Already the missionary torch is being passed to other nations, but it is good to praise God for tens of thousands of American missionaries who gave their lives to take the gospel to the ends of the earth. It was through their work that the church spread in Asia, Africa, and South America.

This was a century, not only for missions, but also for evangelistic crusades. Billy Graham has been perhaps the greatest evangelist since the apostle Paul. Certainly he has preached the good news of the cross and the empty tomb to more souls than any man who has ever lived, and with great results around the globe.

Then there is Bible translation. The work is not yet finished, but the end is almost in sight. Especially through the work of Wycliffe Bible Translators, portions of Scripture have been translated into a couple thousand different languages. This is a reminder that we have been a part, however small, of what God has done in the world in the last century. In spite of all the wars and persecution, God has been building his church.

I did not love the twentieth century, and I did not weep to see it end. But it has confirmed these two great facts: the depravity of man and the grace of God for dying sinners. Though we may not mourn its passing, we may at least write its epitaph: "Where sin increased, grace increased all the more" (Rom. 5:20).[2]

# Part Nine

# CHRISTIANITY TODAY

*The contemporary disaffection with classical evangelicalism,
not to mention the theology of the Bible, has many expressions and
many emphases, not all of which are in agreement with each other,
but there can be little question that the shifting of the sands
that is under way is of major importance.*

DAVID WELLS

IN ANY PARTICULAR CULTURE Christianity is always only one generation away from total elimination. If the rising generation does not come to faith in Jesus Christ, no one will be left to praise the Lord. This is why Asaph had such a passion for telling "the next generation the praiseworthy deeds of the LORD, his power, and the wonders he has done" (Ps. 78:4). He knew that if the people of his generation failed to proclaim God's Word, the legacy of their faith would be lost.

There is also a deeper truth, of course, which is that the church will always persevere. Jesus said, "I will build my church, and the gates of Hades will not overcome it" (Matt. 16:18). By the grace of Jesus Christ and by the power of his Holy Spirit, the church will not fail, but will endure to the end of the age.

To fulfill this promise, however, the church must defend its doctrine. This was a major concern for Peter, Paul, and the other New Testament apostles, who recognized that nothing was a greater threat to the success of their spiritual work than doctrinal declension. They were always trying to preserve the truth of Jesus Christ from theological error.

The defense of Christian orthodoxy is equally important today, when we are witnessing the disintegration of the evangelical consensus. Attacks are coming from every side. There are still vestiges of the old liberal denials of the inerrancy of Scripture, the deity of Jesus Christ, and the efficacy of the atonement. There is a resurgence of Roman Catholicism. There is a new doctrine of God that limits his sovereign knowledge of the future. There is a new perspective on Paul and the law that threatens the great Reformation doctrine of the imputed righteousness of Jesus Christ. There are even some who say that the church age has come to an end.

How do we respond to these and other attacks? By strengthening our grip on the great truths of the gospel. By identifying theological error as error. By relearning the biblical basis for the systematic theology of the church. And by patiently teaching the true doctrine of God and the salvation he offers in Christ.

# 45

# GOD IN CRISIS

Jack Miles is a Pulitzer Prize-winning author who has written two best-selling books about God. The first book was a biography about the God of the Old Testament. The second book has the rather melodramatic title *Christ: A Crisis in the Life of God.*

In this book Miles wrestles with the central question of the gospel: Why did Jesus die on the cross? It is clear from the New Testament that Jesus claimed to be God the Son. He was not merely human, but also divine. It is equally clear that the crucifixion was the major event of his life. But this is shocking. Why should God be the one to die? Miles puts the question like this: "If God had to suffer and die, then God had to inflict suffering and death upon himself. But why would God do this?"[1]

Jack Miles has a simple answer: God needed to atone for his own sins. The crisis in the book's title is the crisis God faced when he realized that the world was in a terrible mess, and that it was partly his fault. God saw the world suffering from the curse he pronounced in the Garden of Eden, and he felt guilty about it. Miles writes: "The disobedience of the first humans was a sin; yet it was not the enormity of that sin but, rather, the ruthlessness of God's curse that brought death into the world. Thus . . . it is God, in the end, who must atone for his vengeful and destructive reaction to their sin by restoring their immortality."

According to Miles, God also recognized that he had failed to keep the terms of his covenant with Israel. In the centuries leading up to the birth of Christ, the Israelites endured great suffering that God did nothing to stop. So Miles imagines God overwhelmed by guilt, struggling to find a way to make things up to his people. He ends up agreeing with Albert Camus that the real reason for the sufferings of the cross was "that [God] himself knew he was not altogether innocent."

This way of looking at the cross makes the crucifixion an act of divine repentance. By dying on the cross, God was confessing his sin of making us go through so much suffering. He was not making atonement for our sin, but for his own. On the cross God was taking personal responsibility for his mistakes. "The world is a great crime," Miles writes, "and someone must be made to pay for it. . . . [T]he New Testament is the story of how someone, the right someone, does pay for it. The ultimately responsible party accepts his responsibility. And once he has paid the price, who else need be blamed, who else need be punished?"

It's not surprising that *Christ: A Crisis in the Life of God* became such a popular book. By blaming God for our problems, it strikes a responsive chord. Ever since the Garden of Eden, human beings have been trying to shift the blame. Adam said to God, "The woman you put here with me—she gave me some fruit from the tree, and I ate it" (Gen. 3:12). Adam tried to fix the blame on Eve for good measure, but his real target was God. After all, God was the one who created the woman, so it must have been his fault.

With the same kind of audacity, Jack Miles attempts to blame God for everything that has happened since. The popularity of his book is partly due to the popularity of its thesis. Who's to blame? God is. It's all his fault, from beginning to end. The ultimate proof is found in the cross, where God died for God's own sin. The cross reveals the truth about God, namely, that he is both divine and guilty.

This is all nonsense, of course. Worse than that, it is blasphemy. The Bible says not one word about God being guilty of anything. On the contrary, it everywhere insists that he cannot be the author of sin. Whatever has gone wrong with the world is properly traced back to humanity's sin. God is not to blame; we are.

Once we properly fix the blame, then we can understand what really did happen on the cross. When Christ was crucified, God was not taking responsibility for his own sin; he was taking the blame for our sin. The New Testament says this over and over again: "God demonstrates his own love for us in this: While we were still sinners, Christ died for us" (Rom. 5:8). Jesus "gave himself for our sins to rescue us from the present evil age" (Gal. 1:4). "He himself bore our sins on the tree, so that we might die to sins and live for righteousness; by his wounds you have been healed" (1 Peter 2:24). Somehow Jack Miles managed to miss these verses, as well as many others that say the same thing.

If we want to understand the New Testament, we need to be clear about what happened on the cross. It is very simple: Christ died for sinners. The Bible says, "Christ died for sins once for all, the righteous for the unrighteous, to bring you to God" (1 Peter 3:18). Jesus Christ was the righteous one. He was not guilty of any sin. He did not deserve to die. Yet die he did, and he did it on our behalf, for our sins.

Our sin—this is what caused the real crisis. It was not a crisis in God, but in our relationship with God. It was our crisis, not his. But God solved it by sending his Son to die in our place.

# 46

## IT'S NOT THE END
## OF THE WORLD

Family Radio, a national network of Christian radio stations, has been faithfully broadcasting Christian radio shows and worship services for years. However, programming changes made in 2001 and issues raised by a significant shift in the theological views of the network's founder, Harold Camping, have jeopardized the network's godly legacy.

In an essay entitled "The End of the External Church," Camping argues that the time has come for faithful Christians to leave the organized church. The essay begins as follows: "The Bible discloses the fact that the last great spiritual event that will occur in this world is that there will be a period of great tribulation which will be immediately followed by the return of Christ and the end of the world." For biblical support, Camping turns to Matthew 24, where Jesus says, "For then shall be great tribulation, such as was not since the beginning of the world to this time, no, nor ever shall be. . . . Immediately after the tribulation of those days shall the sun be darkened, and the moon shall not give her light, and the stars shall fall from heaven, and the powers of the heavens shall be shaken" (Matt. 24:21, 29).

Harold Camping believes that the final tribulation has come. His evidence is sketchy, but it includes the current fascination with signs and wonders, including the charismatic practice of "being slain in the Spirit." Camping views this phenomenon as the last Satanic sign foretold in Revelation 13. He also notes that in the present era we have unprecedented opportunities to spread the gospel around the world. Surely this means that we are getting close to the end of history, when the full number of the elect will be saved.

If it's the end of the world, then what should Christians do? Harold Camping thinks we should leave the church. In his view, "Satan has occupied the churches and has become victorious over the saints." The evangelical pulpit has become a "high place," like the ones where people offered pagan sacrifices in the Old Testament, and thus it needs to be torn down.

Camping takes Matthew 24:15–16 as a command for Christians today: "When ye therefore shall see the abomination of desolation . . . stand in the holy place . . . then . . . flee into the mountains." In this verse Jesus was telling his disciples what to do when Jerusalem was destroyed. However, on Camping's reading, this verse commands Christians to flee the church. Here is his conclusion: "No longer are you to be under the spiritual rulership of the church. . . . God is finished with the era of churches being used of God to evangelize. . . . We must remove ourself [sic] from the church. . . . [T]he church era has come to an end and the church no longer has any divine authority."

What shall we say in response? First, that it is always a risky business to predict the end of the world. Harold Camping should know, because his own prediction that it would end in 1994 is now history. We know Jesus is coming soon, because the Bible tells us to expect his return at any moment. But we don't know exactly when. Jesus said, "No one knows about that day or hour, not even the angels in heaven, nor the Son, but only the Father" (Matt. 24:36).

Even if we did know, this would be no time to panic. Still less would it be a time to give up on the church, which God has promised to endure until the very end (see Matt. 16:18). Rather, it is a time to live stable, godly lives, which always includes remaining committed to the local church. As Peter told the early Christians, "The day of the Lord will come like a thief. The heavens will disappear with a roar; the elements will be destroyed by fire, and the earth and everything in it will be laid bare. Since everything will be destroyed in this way, what kind of people ought you to be? You ought to live holy and godly lives as you look forward to the day of God and speed its coming" (2 Peter 3:10–12).

The current controversy also shows how important it is to know how to interpret the Bible. Harold Camping's essay repeatedly makes elementary errors in hermeneutics, or biblical interpretation. In particular, it takes prophecies concerning Jerusalem that have already been fulfilled and mistakenly assumes that somehow they will be fulfilled again in the church.

We greet these developments with sadness and Christian concern. Family Radio is at risk of squandering its rich legacy of gospel ministry. We believe that Harold Camping's teaching about the church is not only false, but also dangerous, because it encourages people to leave the community God has ordained for our growth in grace. It is our prayer that one day the network will reaffirm the importance of the visible church, which everywhere in the New Testament is viewed as essential to God's plan for saving the world in Jesus Christ.

# 47

# THE CLOSING OF GOD

What does God know, and when does he know it? This was the question addressed at the 53rd annual meetings of the Evangelical Theological Society (or ETS). The Society is made up of Bible scholars and theologians from across America. Most of the members teach in evangelical colleges and seminaries, or in other academic institutions, although many pastors also attend.

The 2001 conference was entitled "Defining Evangelicalism's Boundaries." The title reflected the fact that the Society was engaged—some would say embroiled—in a significant doctrinal controversy concerning the knowledge of God.

During the past decade a group of theologians has begun to advocate a new doctrine of God known as "Open Theism" (or "the Openness of God"). So far discussions about this new theology have been limited primarily to academic theologians. But like all false teaching, eventually Open Theism will begin to infect the church. Indeed, debates concerning Open Theism have appeared in the pages of *Christianity Today,* and a number of popular books on the subject have been published.

What is Open Theism? It is the belief that God does not have exhaustive knowledge of the future. While there are many things that God does know, he cannot know human decisions in advance. He has chosen to limit his sovereignty in such a way that he does not know what we will choose to do. In fact, sometimes he is surprised by the choices we make. Only in this way, Open Theists argue, can human beings have meaningful freedom.

There are many Bible passages that speak of God repenting (e.g. 1 Sam. 15:35), grieving (e.g. Gen. 6:6), or even changing his mind (e.g. Jer. 18:8, 10). According to Open Theism, in order for these passages to be true, God must be vulnerable to his creatures. It must be possible for him to be influenced by our actions—even to suffer from them—in ways that he did not expect.

The issue confronting the Evangelical Theological Society is whether it will allow its members to teach this new doctrine of God. The ETS doctrinal statement does not address the divine attributes directly. It only requires members to affirm biblical inerrancy and the doctrine of the Trinity. The reason the Society gets away with such a short doctrinal statement is that it has enjoyed a high degree of consensus about the main tenets of evangelical theology. But now that consensus is threatened by a new doctrine of God.

Many of the papers in 2001 dealt in one way or another with Open Theism. On the last night there was an extended debate, after which the ETS passed the following resolution: "We believe the Bible clearly teaches that God has complete, accurate and infallible knowledge of all events past, present and future including all future decisions and actions of free moral agents." For now the passage of this resolution has little practical effect, especially since only seventy percent of the membership voted in its favor. What remains to be seen is whether in coming years the Society will vote to deny membership to Open Theists. This is by no means certain, since an eighty percent majority is required to amend the standards for membership.

I voted in favor of the resolution because I believe that the denial of God's foreknowledge is heresy, in the proper sense of the term. Open Theism is contrary to the orthodox teaching of the Christian church.

There are many ways to refute Open Theism. One is to list some of the passages of Scripture that clearly speak of God's foreknowledge. The apostle Paul assured the Romans that "those God foreknew he also predestined to be conformed to the likeness of his Son" (Rom. 8:29). Peter addressed the early Christians as "God's elect . . . who have been chosen according to the foreknowledge of God the Father" (1 Peter 1:1–2). But what is true for us in salvation is true of everything that happens in the world: it is all according to God's plan and purpose. As God said through the prophet Isaiah, "I am God, and there is no other; I am God, and there is none like me. I make known the end from the beginning, from ancient times, what is still to come" (Isa. 46:9–10). Or again, "Who then is like me? Let him proclaim it. Let him declare . . . what is yet to come" (Isa. 44:7). What distinguishes the true God from his rivals is that he alone knows the future.

Another way to refute Open Theism is to explain what the Bible means when it says that God repents, or changes his mind. Such statements are *anthropopaphisms.* That is to say, they express God's emotions in human terms. They are similar to *anthropomorphisms,* in which God's attributes are compared to human body parts. The Scripture speaks, for example, of God's "right hand and his holy arm" (Ps. 98:1). Obviously, God does not have a bicep. These are simply manners of speech intended to reveal something true about God in terms that we can understand. But we would be mistaken to conclude from these metaphors that God has the same kind of body that we have. We need to understand the biblical statements about God grieving and repenting in the same way. These expressions help us understand our relationship with God, but they do not mean that God experiences emotion the same way that we do. Still less does it mean that his knowledge is limited.

A third way to refute Open Theism is to consider its implications for biblical inerrancy. The Bible contains thousands of prophecies about the future, many of which have already been fulfilled. Now when God made those prophecies, did he know for certain that they would come true? According to Open Theism, he could not have known, because nearly every biblical prophecy depends partly on the actions of human beings. For example, God promised to bless all the nations of the world through Abraham. But Open Theists say that when God tested Abraham on the mountain in the sacrifice of his son, he didn't know whether Abraham would pass the test. In that case, God's promise was nothing more than a prediction.

Or consider a more serious example. Consistent Open Theists deny that God the Father knew whether God the Son would resist the temptation to avoid the cross. Yet the Scripture says that Jesus was crucified "by God's set purpose and foreknowledge" (Acts 2:23).

Finally, the denial of God's foreknowledge has obvious implications for the future. How can we be certain that God will deliver on all his promises for the end of history? If the future is the combined result of what God and his creatures decide to do, then how can we be sure that God's forecast will come true? The denial of God's complete foreknowledge is not simply false, but also heretical, and we should pray for God to defend his church against it.[1]

# SAINT KATHARINE?

On October 1, 2000, Pope John Paul II canonized Philadelphia's second official saint: Mother Katharine Drexel (1858–1955). Saint Katharine, as Roman Catholics will now call her, was the founder of the Sisters of the Blessed Sacrament (1891). Despite the fact that she inherited the Drexel family's fabulous banking fortune, she took a vow of poverty in order to serve African and Native Americans. By the time of her death at the age of 96, Mother Drexel had disbursed some $20 million to charitable causes, using her inheritance to establish more than 200 Catholic missions and dozens of schools for American Indians and African Americans.

It is not easy to become a Catholic saint, so how did Katharine qualify? Obviously, in order even to be considered, she had to be known for good works. And so she was. Katharine cared for the poor and the needy of Philadelphia. She also lived in poverty herself, mending her own clothes and traveling by third-class rail. Long before the Civil Rights movement, she had a special concern for racial reconciliation. In addition to the usual vows of poverty, chastity, and obedience, Katharine also promised "To be the mother and servant of the Indian and Negro races according to the rule of the Sisters of the Blessed Sacrament; and not to undertake any work which would lead to the neglect or abandonment of the Indian and Colored races."

Yet for all her many virtues, Katharine Drexel never could have been canonized without performing at least two certifiable, posthumous miracles. In 1975 a teenager reported that his hearing was restored after praying to Katharine from his hospital bed. Medical experts discovered that a bone in the boy's ear that had been dissolved by a previous infection had inexplicably grown back. Then in 1993 the family of a one-year-old claimed that in answer to the prayers offered in the name of Saint Katharine, their daughter was healed of nerve deafness. After conducting a thorough investigation, a panel of Vatican doctors declared that both of these healings were undoubtedly miraculous.

It is easy to understand why the Roman Catholic Church wants to honor their dead. As the Scripture says, "Blessed are the dead who die in the Lord" (Rev. 14:13). It is also easy to see the value of emulating outstanding Christians in their practical godliness. We are called to care for the needy, to love mercy, and to break the cords of injustice. The work that Katharine Drexel did among the urban poor is the kind of service that Christ demands of all his disciples.

Yet her canonization also shows what is wrong with the Catholic notion of sainthood. To begin with, there is no biblical support for the idea of praying to the dead. The Bible teaches that "there is one God and one mediator between God and men, the man Christ Jesus" (1 Tim. 2:5). If that is true, then offering intercession to someone like Katharine Drexel is at best unnecessary, and at worst blasphemy.

Then there is the issue of the healings themselves. Were they genuine miracles? I don't know. Maybe they were, but if so, then God should get the credit for them, and not some dead person, however virtuous. One is reminded of the apostle Paul, who rebuked the people of Lystra for trying to worship him after he performed a miracle, saying, "We too are only men, human like you" (Acts 14:15).

The process of becoming a saint is also open to corruption. Candidates go through a careful screening process that involves reading letters, conducting interviews, and studying medical records. Sometimes—as in the recent case of Pius IX—the saint's corpse has to be exhumed for evidence. However, in order for all of this to be successful, it pays to know someone at the Vatican. In the words of one professor from Notre Dame, "It helps a lot if you have connections in Rome. And it helps a lot if you can come up with the bucks." Perhaps this explains why some Catholics have returned to selling relics, like they did in the Middle Ages. It may also explain why sainthood has become a growth industry in Rome: The current pontiff has canonized nearly 300 saints.

These problems aside, the real difficulty with making someone like Katharine Drexel a saint is that it gives the impression that there are two kinds of Christians. There are ordinary Christians, and then there are saints. However, the New Testament refers to all God's people as saints, even the ones who seem more like sinners. So, for example, when the apostle Paul wrote letters to Christians in Ephesus and Philippi, he addressed them as "the saints in Christ Jesus."

During the centuries that followed, it was customary for Christians to refer to one another as saints. This preserved an important truth namely, that every Christian is holy. The word "saint" (*hagios*) simply means "holy one." The reason we are "holy ones" is not because we are particularly holy ourselves, but because Jesus Christ is holy, and we are connected to him by faith.

A good place to see what the Bible means when it talks about saints is Paul's first letter to the Corinthians. The Corinthians were not very holy. In fact, they were guilty of pride, adultery, dissension, and a host of other sins. Nevertheless, Paul addressed them as "those sanctified in Christ Jesus and called to be holy" (1 Cor. 1:2). As unholy as they were, the Corinthians were made holy by their faith-connection to Jesus Christ. Later Paul would tell them: "you are in Christ Jesus, who . . . is our . . . holiness" (1 Cor. 1:30).

The saintliness of the saints, therefore, does not depend on their own personal holiness. It depends on the holiness of Jesus Christ, received by faith. Rather than being a sort of lifetime achievement award for super-Christians, sainthood is the high privilege of every sinner who trusts in Christ for forgiveness. We cannot be certain if Katharine Drexel was a saint in the biblical sense of the word. But if she was, it was only by faith.[1]

# UNITED PRESBYTERIANS DIVIDED

The PCUSA was in the news during the summer of 2001 because its General Assembly voted 317–208 to rescind its "fidelity and chastity rule" for ministers, and specifically to allow practicing homosexuals to be ordained as pastors. Formerly the denomination maintained the biblical position that the only proper context for sexual intimacy is in the marriage of one man to one woman for life (see Gen. 2:24; Matt. 5:31–32). To quote from the old policy, "Those who are called to office in the church are to lead a life in obedience to Scripture and . . . to live either in fidelity within the covenant of marriage between a man and a woman, or chastity in singleness."

Over the past decade the issue of gay clergy has become increasingly divisive in the PCUSA. Now the battleground shifts from the national level to the local church, because in order for the assembly's decision to become part of the *Book of Order*, it must be ratified by a majority of regional presbyteries.

Although gay ordination has generated the most attention, the PCUSA took another vote of even more far-reaching significance. A group of conservative Presbyterians asked the denomination to endorse a statement affirming salvation in Christ alone. To use the specific language of the proposal, Jesus is the "singular saving Lord." Unfortunately, this motion was defeated, and a substitute was adopted. Delegates agreed to confess "the unique authority of Jesus Christ as Lord," but they were unwilling to say that Jesus is the only way of salvation. In the words of a PCUSA minister from Chicago, "What's the big deal about Jesus?"

This attitude is becoming increasingly common, even among Christians who call themselves evangelicals. Often the idea is that somehow God can save people through other religions. As the assembly said, "Although we do not know the limits of God's grace and pray for the salvation of those who may never come to know Christ, *for us* the assurance of salvation is found in confessing Christ and trusting him alone" (emphasis added).

This leaves open the possibility that people can be saved in some other way. Jesus is *our* Savior, but maybe other people can be saved in some other way. However, the Bible says, "Salvation is found in no one else, for there is no other name under heaven given to men by which we must be saved" (Acts 4:12). Consider, too, how odd it is to pray for people to be saved without ever coming to know Christ. This is what salvation is: It is knowing Christ. Thus it would be much better to pray that those who do not know Christ would come to know him, and in this way be saved.

In short, the General Assembly was unable to give an unequivocal answer to the question Jesus asked his disciples: "Who do you say that I am?" This failure moved evangelicals to action. The *Presbyterian Layman* decried what it viewed as "an apostate assembly," and conservative churches in the PCUSA have formed what is called the Confessing Church Movement.

Together these churches urge presbyteries, sessions, and individual church members to join other faithful believers in confessing:

> That Jesus Christ alone is Lord of all and the way of salvation.
> That holy Scripture is the triune God's revealed Word, the Church's only infallible rule of faith and life.

That God's people are called to holiness in all aspects of life; this includes honoring the sanctity of marriage between a man and a woman, the only relationship within which sexual activity is permitted by Scripture.

The doctrines that the Confessing Church Movement defends are cardinal doctrines of the Christian faith: the person and work of Jesus Christ, the way of salvation, the authority of the Bible. This may be the last chance for these doctrines in the PCUSA. Then again, it may be too late already. *The Washington Times* reported that a majority of PCUSA pastors believe that a denominational breakup is inevitable, at least by the year 2050.

It is not surprising that the PCUSA now finds itself embroiled in what the current moderator calls "Presbyterian civil war." Many of those caught up in the fight are our friends. There are many solid, Bible-teaching PCUSA churches. We should pray for them as they defend biblical ethics and an orthodox theology of salvation, and perhaps in some cases as they begin to consider a new denomination to call home.[1]

## 50

# THE WORD MADE FRESH?

As someone born and raised in the evangelical church, I take a special interest in the future of evangelicalism in America. But what exactly is an evangelical, anyway?

Today that is precisely the question. In its most basic sense, an evangelical is someone who believes the gospel—the good news about salvation through the death and resurrection of Jesus Christ. Although the term is biblical, it was first used to describe a group of people during the Protestant Reformation in Germany. In America "evangelical" is generally used to describe Christians who believe that the Bible is the inerrant Word of God, who defend orthodox doctrines of the person and work of Jesus Christ (especially his deity and substitutionary atonement), who hold that a person must be born again to be saved, and who have a personal relationship with Jesus Christ. These are some of the central doctrines of the evangelical church.

However, in recent years there have been more and more disputes about the boundaries of evangelical orthodoxy. Who counts as an evangelical, and who doesn't? Who's in and who's out? The very fact that we are having these debates is a sign that evangelicalism is losing its way.

From time to time I have pointed out some of the doctrines that are now under attack. I fear that some evangelicals are losing their grip on biblical inerrancy, the belief that the Bible does not and cannot err. Others are relaxing their stand on Jesus as the only way to God. Still others are starting to downplay the importance or even deny the validity of the evangelical doctrine of justification by grace alone, through faith alone. Then there is a fresh assault on the doctrine of God. According to the view commonly known as "Open Theism," God does not have complete foreknowledge of the future.

It is in this context that we are confronted with a new theological statement called "The Word Made Fresh: A Call for a Renewal of the Evangelical Spirit." The document is signed by dozens of Bible scholars and theologians from leading evangelical colleges, seminaries, and publishing houses, including prominent leaders in the movement sometimes known as post-conservative evangelicalism.

These men and women are trying to push the biblical and theological boundaries. Fortunately, they oppose "unfettered theological experimentation and accommodation to culture that threatens the gospel of Jesus Christ." Yet their primary concern is to make sure they have the freedom to explore creative new directions in theology and to "challenge received evangelical tradition." They prize "genuine diversity and fresh reflection." They favor dialogue and debate that will lead to "constructive theological proposals." To that end, they "deplore a present tendency among some evangelicals to define the boundaries of evangelical faith and life too narrowly." "Some claimants to the evangelical heritage," they say, "appear to be falling back into some of the more onerous attitudes of fundamentalism." Thus they warn against "condemnations and threats of exclusion" that disrupt Christian community and quench the Spirit.

It would be interesting to know exactly whom they have in mind. Who is making these threats? Who is propagating what the writers disparage as "rigid definitions of evangelicalism" that result in alienation and exclusion? Possibly these remarks are directed against the opponents of Open Theism. At present there is a movement within the Evangelical Theological Society to deny fellowship to members who advocate the open view of God. But maybe "The Word Made Fresh" has someone else in mind, like evangelicals who criticize the new gender-neutral Bible translation known as the TNIV: Today's New International Version. Possibly they object to the rigorous Reformation theology promoted by the Alliance of Confessing Evangelicals. Or maybe they have someone else in mind entirely. The statement is short on specifics, so it's hard to tell.

The question is whether evangelical theology needs greater clarity, as I believe, or greater openness to new directions in doctrine. The problem with "The Word Made Fresh" is that rather than stating what it is that we believe, it advocates theological innovation. Noticeably absent is any clear statement of evangelical essentials. True, the statement refers broadly to the Lordship of Jesus Christ and the authority of the Bible. But nothing is said about the Trinity, biblical inerrancy, the substitutionary atonement, the new birth, or many other cardinal tenets of evangelical theology. Instead, it is all about "the exploration of new ideas" (which are left unspecified).

This is very different from what we find in the New Testament, where the most important theological task of the church is to defend Christian orthodoxy from error and novelty. The apostle Paul was forever saying things like "keep the pattern of sound teaching" (2 Tim. 1:13), and "guard the good deposit that was entrusted to you" (2 Tim. 1:14). For the apostles, the important thing in theology was not coming up with new proposals, but proclaiming the "faith that was once for all entrusted to the saints" (Jude 3).

I find myself in agreement with what "The Word Made Fresh" says about having theological discussions that are "characterized by an irenic, Christlike spirit of love toward those with whom we disagree and a cautious openness to the reform of tradition as the Spirit leads us to fresh understandings of the Word that are even more faithful to the entirety of God's revelation." Yet I find myself in disagreement with what the statement says about what the church needs today. In my view, what the evangelical church needs is not greater ambiguity about the boundaries of Christian orthodoxy, but greater clarity. The church can only fulfill its mission when its pastors and teachers have a firm grip on their doctrine of Scripture, their doctrine of God, and their doctrines of the person and work of Jesus Christ.

This is one of the reasons why the church needs its creeds and confessions. These summaries of biblical truth guard us against the temptation to be trendy in our theology. Without them, we are vulnerable to all kinds of doctrinal change that will lead to error. With them, we know where the boundaries are. And boundaries are both useful and necessary. They are not arbitrary, but have been established by the church's careful reflection on the Word of God. Observing them is an exercise in theological humility.

Of course we need to study God's Word, and of course this will lead to fresh theological insight. But we can and we must do this without blurring the boundaries of evangelical orthodoxy.

# NOTES

### Introduction

1. Louis Berkhof, *Systematic Theology* (Grand Rapids, Mich.: Eerdmans, 1941), 434.

### Chapter 1: Campus Courtship

1. David Gilmore, et al., quoted in Maggie Gallagher, "Where Have All the Grownups Gone?" *Family Policy* 13, no. 4 (July–August 2000): 1.

### Chapter 2: In Praise of Modesty

1. William Lamb, "Haverford College to Let Women, Men Share Rooms," *Philadelphia Inquirer,* March 31, 2000, A1.

2. Daniel P. Moloney, "Eroticism Unbound," *First Things,* February 1999, 15.

### Chapter 4: Keep Your Eye on the Dad

1. David Blankenhorn, *Fatherless America* (New York: HarperCollins, 1995).

2. Ibid., 1.

### Chapter 5: A Mother's Touch

1. Richard Lacayo, "A Tale of Two Brothers," *Time,* April 22, 1996, 44–50 (p. 46).

2. Dorothy Kunhardt, *Pat the Bunny* (New York: Golden Books).

## Chapter 6: Domestic Partners

1. John Street, quoted in a Philadelphia Urban Coalition newsletter dated June 12, 1996.

2. Gregory Koukl, *Solid Ground* (March/April, 1999): 4.

3. Act 124, Section 1704 (1996), 21–22.

## Chapter 8: The Team That Didn't Have a Prayer

1. Sources for this chapter include Geraldine Sealey, "Court Bans Pre-Game Prayer," abcnews.com, June 19, 2000; Joan Biskupic, "School prayer rejected" and other articles in *USA Today*, June 20, 2000; Edward Walsh and Bill Miller, "Praying before playing is barred," *Philadelphia Inquirer*, June 20, 2000, A1; and Timothy Roche, "Too Much Like a Prayer?" *Time*, September 18, 2000, 59.

## Chapter 10: Should I Pray When I Score a Touchdown?

1. Westminster Confession of Faith, V.i.

## Chapter 11: The Brooklyn Dodgers and the Third Use of the Law

1. John Devaney, *The Greatest Cardinals of Them All* (New York: Putnam, 1968), 86.

2. Bob Broeg, *Stan Musial* (New York: Doubleday, 1964), 58.

3. Augustine, quoted in J. I. Packer, *Concise Theology* (InterVarsity: Downers Grove, Ill.: 1993), 94.

## Chapter 12: Feeling Sleepy?

1. *Philadelphia Inquirer*, March 28, 2001, A4.

## Part 3: Science and Technology

1. Johannes Kepler, quoted in Nancy R. Pearcey and Charles B. Thaxton, *The Soul of Science: Christian Faith and Natural Philosophy* (Wheaton, Ill.: Crossway, 1994), 23.

## Chapter 13: RU Crazy?

1. Most of the information in this chapter comes from Nancy Gibbs, "The Abortion Pill," *Time,* October 9, 2000, 40–49. The linguistic argument that the womb is sacred space comes from Peter J. Leithart, "Attacking the Tabernacle," *First Things,* November 1999, 15–16.

## Chapter 14: Intelligent Design

1. Quoted in Phillip E. Johnson, "The Unraveling of Scientific Materialism," *First Things* 77 (November, 1997): 22–25.

2. For more information on Intelligent Design, read Phillip Johnson's *Darwin on Trial,* Michael Behe's *Darwin's Black Box,* or William Dembski's article "The Intelligent Design Movement," which appeared in the Spring 1998 issue of *Cosmic Pursuit.* See also the Discovery Institute website: www.discovery.org.

## Chapter 15: The Dopamine Made Me Do It

1. N. D. Volkow, G. J. Wang, M. W. Fischman, et al., "Relationship between subjective effects of cocaine and dopamine transporter occupancy," *Nature,* vol. 386 (April 24, 1997), 827–30.

2. Tom Wolfe, "Sorry, But Your Soul Just Died," *Forbes,* vol. 158, no. 13 (December 2, 1996).

## Chapter 16: The God of the Genome

1. Information for this chapter comes from the July 3, 2000, issue of *Time* and the June 27, 2002, "Science Times" section of the *New York Times.* Stephen Master, who is a Ph.D. candidate in molecular biology at the University of Pennsylvania, helped to clarify a number of points made in this essay.

## Part 4: Social Issues

1. Martin Luther, *The Large Catechism* (Philadelphia: Fortress, 1959), 61.

## Chapter 19: The Color Line

1. Census analysis and quoted material come from Laurent Belsie, *The Christian Science Monitor,* March 14, 2001.

## Chapter 20: Face to Face

1. Information for this chapter comes from various articles in *Time, Newsweek,* and from the Physicians for Human Rights web page (www.phrusa.org).

## Chapter 21: The Lion, the Witch, and the Boardroom

1. See Marvin Olasky, "Off with his Head," *World,* June 16, 2001, 30–36.

2. Judith Shulevitz, "Don't Mess with Aslan," *The New York Times Book Review,* August 26, 2001, 27.

3. Martin Moynihan, ed. and trans., *The Latin Letters of C. S. Lewis* (Wheaton, Ill.: Crossway, 1987), 42.

## Chapter 22: Dr. Phil

1. This, and other quotes are from Phillip C. McGraw, *Self Matters* (New York: Simon and Schuster, 2001).

2. From Ralph Waldo Emerson's famous essay "Self-Reliance."

## Chapter 23: Heroin Chic

1. Roy H. Campbell, "Just say, 'Oh No!' " *Philadelphia Inquirer* (October 8, 1996), F1.

2. Janice M. Horowitz and Lina Lofaro, "What ever happened to 'cherries in the snow'?" *Time,* vol. 148, no. 13 (September 16, 1996), 28.

3. Peter Gould, quoted in Campbell, F1.

## Chapter 25: Good News, Bible Clubs

1. Jordan Lorence, Alliance Defense Fund, quoted in *Christianity Today,* August 6, 2001, 24.

2. Unless otherwise indicated, all quotations come from Good News Club v. Milford Central School, No. 99–2036, argued February 28, 2001; decided June 11, 2001.

**Chapter 26: A Not-So Charitable Choice?**

1. Information for this chapter comes from a January 29, 2001, news report from CNN and from John J. DiIulio's column in the February 14, 2001, issue of the *Wall Street Journal*: "Know Us by Our Works: Give Faith a Chance to solve Society's Problems."

**Chapter 34: Star of Bethlehem**

1. Patrick Moore, *The Star of Publishing* (Bristol, U.K.: Canopus, 2001).

2. Craig Chester, "The Star of Bethlehem," *Imprimis* 22, no. 12 (December 1993).

**Part 7: The Bible**

1. James Montgomery Boice and Paul Steven Jones, *Hymns for a Modern Reformation* (Philadelphia: Tenth Presbyterian Church, 2000), 10.

**Chapter 37: The New NIV**

1. For further reading, consult D. A. Carson, *The Inclusive Language Debate: A Plea for Realism* (Grand Rapids: Baker, 1998); Mark L. Strauss, *Distorting Scripture? The Challenge of Bible Translation and Gender Accuracy* (Downers Grove, Ill.: InterVarsity, 1998); and especially Vern Poythress and Wayne Grudem, *The Gender-Neutral Bible Controversy: Muting the Masculinity of God's Words* (Nashville: Broadman & Holman, 2000).

**Chapter 38: The Prayer of Jabez**

1. Bruce Wilkinson, *The Prayer of Jabez: Breaking Through to the Blessed Life* (Sisters, Ore.: Multnomah, 2000), 44.

2. Ibid., 27.

3. Ibid., 7.

## Chapter 39: The Box for His Brother's Bones

1. Information for this chapter comes from Gordon Govier, "Stunning New Evidence of Jesus," *Christianity Today,* November 18, 2002; Hillary Mayell, "Burial Box May Be That of Jesus's Brother, Expert Says," Internet posting by *National Geographic News* (October 21, 2002); Jeffrey L. Sheler, "A Discovery and a Debate," *U. S. News & World Report,* November 4, 2002; and David Van Biema, "The Brother of Jesus?" *Time,* November 4, 2002.

## Part 8: Church History

1. George M. Marsden, *Jonathan Edwards: A Life* (New Haven, Conn.: Yale University Press, 2003), 488–89.

## Chapter 40: The Church Mothers

1. Quoted in J. N. D. Kelly, *Golden Mouth: The Story of John Chrysostom—Ascetic, Preacher, Bishop* (Grand Rapids: Baker, 1995), 7.

2. Jerome, "Epistle 127," quoted in Christopher A. Hall, *Reading Scripture with the Church Fathers* (Downers Grove, Ill.: InterVarsity, 1998), 44.

3. Jerome, "Epistle 108," quoted in Hall, 44.

4. Palladius, quoted in Hall, 45.

5. Quoted in Hall, 46.

6. For more information about the Church Mothers, consult Elizabeth A. Clark, *Women in the Early Church* (Collegeville, Minn.: Liturgical Press, 1983).

## Chapter 41: Diet of Worms

1. *Luther's Works,* eds. Jaroslav Pelikan (vols. 1–30) and Helmut T. Lehmann (vols. 31–55) (Minneapolis: Fortress and Concordia, 1955–76), 34:336–37.

2. Ibid.

3. For the full account of Luther's trial, see *Luther's Works* 32:103–31.

4. *Luther's Works* 53:223.

5. Historical details for this chapter were drawn chiefly from Mark A. Noll, *Turning Points: Decisive Moments in the History of Christianity* (Grand Rapids: Baker, 1997), 151–74; among the best biographies of Luther is Roland H. Bainton, *Here I Stand: A Life of Martin Luther* (New York: Abingdon, 1950).

## Chapter 42: The Westminster Assembly

1. For more information about the history of the Westminster Assembly, see William Barker, *Puritan Profiles* (Fearn, Ross-shire: Mentor, 1996), and John L. Carson and David W. Hall, eds., *To Glorify and Enjoy God* (Carlisle, Pa.: Banner of Truth, 1994). For help studying the Westminster Standards themselves, use A. A. Hodge, *The Confession of Faith* (Carlisle, Pa.: Banner of Truth, 1958), and Thomas Vincent, *The Shorter Catechism Explained from Scripture* (Carlisle, Pa.: Banner of Truth, 1980).

## Chapter 43: The Great Awakening

1. "A History of the Work of Redemption," in *The Great Awakening*, eds. Alan Heimert and Perry Miller (Indianapolis: Bobbs-Merrill, 1967), 21.

2. "Account of the Revival at Lyme," in *Great Awakening*, 37.

## Chapter 44: The American Century

1. Robert Conquest, *Reflections on a Ravaged Century* (New York: Norton, 1999).

2. For more information consult "The Church in the Contemporary World," in Howard F. Vos, *Exploring Church History* (Nashville: Thomas Nelson, 1994), 143–206.

## Chapter 45: God in Crisis

1. All quotations (except those from the Bible) come from Jack Miles, *Christ: A Crisis in the Life of God* (New York: Alfred A. Knopf, 2001).

## Chapter 47: The Closing of God

1. For a helpful critique of Open Theism, see Bruce Ware, *God's Lesser Glory* (Wheaton, Ill.: Crossway, 2001) or John M. Frame, *No Other God* (Phillipsburg, N.J.: P&R, 2001).

## Chapter 48: Saint Katharine?

1. Biographical information about Katharine Drexel comes from articles in the *Philadelphia Inquirer* and the January 11, 2000 issue of *U.S. News & World Report.* For a brief summary of Catholic beliefs on sainthood, see Matthew F. Kohmescher, *Catholicism Today: A Survey of Catholic Belief and Practice* (New York: Paulist, 1999), 205–9.

## Chapter 49: United Presbyterians Divided

1. For further teaching on the uniqueness of Christ and his saving work, see the booklet from Crossway entitled *Is Jesus the Only Way?* by Philip Graham Ryken (Wheaton, Ill.: Crossway, 1999).

# INDEX OF NAMES

# INDEX OF SCRIPTURE

**Philip G. Ryken** (D.Phil., Oxford University) is senior minister of Tenth Presbyterian Church, Philadelphia and Bible teacher for the Alliance of Confessing Evangelicals, appearing on the radio program Every Last Word. He has written more than fourteen books including *My Father's World: Meditations on Christianity and Culture* and *City on a Hill: Reclaiming the Biblical Pattern for the Church in the 21st Century*. Dr. Ryken has also edited *Tenth Presbyterian Church of Philadelphia: 175 Years of Thinking and Acting Biblically*. He coedited *Give Praise to God: A Vision for Reforming Worship*.